■■■ My Mother's Rules

My Mother's Rules

A Practical Guide to Becoming an Emotional Genius

LYNN TOLER

CHICAGO

Printed in United States of America

Library of Congress Cataloging-in-Publication Data
Toler, Lynn.
    My mother's rules: a practical guide to becoming an emotional
genius / by Lynn Toler.
        p. cm.
    Summary: "Autobiography of Judge Lynn Toler describing her
sometimes difficult upbringing and the life-lessons she learned from
her mother"—Provided by publisher.
    ISBN-13: 978-1-932841-22-0 (pbk.)
    ISBN-10: 1-932841-22-9 (pbk.)
    1. Emotional intelligence. 2. Emotions. 3. Conduct of life.
4. Toler, Lynn. 5. Mothers and daughters—United States—Biography.
6. Judges—Ohio—Cleveland—Biography. I. Title.

BF576.T65 2007
152.4--dc22

                              2006021572

            17 16 15 14 13   23 24 25 26 27
Agate books are available in bulk at discount prices. For more
information, go to
Agatepublishing.com

CONTENTS

To my sister,
Kathy

ACKNOWLEDGMENTS AND AUTHOR'S NOTE

I'd like to thank Jeff Lucier for reading the first draft, which could not have been easy, and giving me such great feedback.

I'd also like to thank Jayne and Chris Eiben for all of their help. They gave me great direction and unbelievable support.

Thanks, too, to Matthew Hatchadorian. He was the first one to tell me I should run for judge.

And last, but certainly not least, I'd like to thank my husband, Eric Mumford, whose unwavering and occasionally irrational belief in me helped me turn so many of my dreams into reality.

In this book, I tell many stories based to some extent in experiences I have had serving on the bench. Although they are all a matter of public record, I massaged the facts in order to avoid causing any undue embarrassment. Thrown chairs became broken windows; brothers became cousins; and names most definitely were changed. However, I took special care not to change the instructive dynamics of these situations.

▶ *One:*

The Proper Emotion

No one really got excited until the day they found me sitting in the closet.

"Lots of kids play in the closet," I told my mother, suggesting that she may have simply misinterpreted what she saw.

"Sitting in the closet wasn't the problem," she said. "We only started worrying when we couldn't get you out." My mother then paused, as she sometimes does, for a little dramatic effect. Lowering her voice and leaning into me, she said, "Do you realize you told me you couldn't get out because it wasn't safe?"

That was the comment, I now understand, that set off my mother's alarm and sent me to the doctor so Mom could face her greatest fear.

|||

While I admit the closet thing seems a bit odd, I do have an explanation. Possessed of a predisposition to panic, I have never been a brave soul. Wild, irrational worry comes naturally to me. I was, it appears, *designed* that way. I think it is in my genes.

My father, on the other hand, was a little nuts—a man who, had he been born in this day and age, most surely would have been medicated. Volatile, unrelenting, an incident poised to occur, Daddy was an ongoing event. At our house, a mispronounced word could have us running for our lives. A dirty carpet could lead to gunplay.

This, of course, was not the ideal environment in which to raise a flighty kid. Unlike my sister, Kathy, a sturdier child who took our father in stride, I could not separate the things Daddy did from the way the rest of the world worked. I thought the entire universe rocked and rolled with the same abandon as did our living room, an outlook which made camping out with clothes seem like a reasonable thing to do.

I would, however, like to point out that I am quite recovered now. I haven't had the urge to reside with coats and boots for years. In fact, my current state of mental health is a source of great pride for me. Though once unable to rationalize my way out of a closet, I am now a woman to whom others go for good advice and calm. Once the first to run when trouble arose, I now regularly chase storms.

How did I do it, you ask? What wisdom did I acquire that not only got me out of the closet, but now allows me to feel at ease almost anywhere I go?

Neither therapy nor meditation authored my eventual calm. Pop psychology was not employed, nor were years of getting the real thing. The answer is simply this: I have an extraordinary mother, a woman who is master of an art most people don't even see as a skill. Toni Toler, the woman who brought me into this world—not once, I contend, but twice—is an incredible emotional manager. She has this amazing ability to step away from herself and *decide* how she will feel. It is a talent most people fail to recognize, not to mention understand. It is also a talent, I now know, she purposely passed on to me.

My mother's unusual gift is a bit difficult to describe. In fact, I did not fully understand it myself until I became a judge. That's right—the little girl who once took up residence in a closet eventually took the bench. For eight years I ran a municipal court, a place often referred to as the court of the common man. Municipal court is the judicial home of traffic tickets, evictions, and barking dogs. It's where people go to discuss bad hair cuts, loud parties, and unpaid rent. Feuding neighbors are often sent there to explain the lump on the other guy's head. In short, a municipal court is where regular people go when they get caught doing irregular things.

Of course, it isn't all small stuff. Municipal courts see a lot of domestic violence, drunk driving, and assault charges. Every once in a while we'll see negligent or vehicular homicide cases as well. But these things do not take up the bulk of a municipal judge's day. For the most part, municipal judges see familiar misfortune and commonplace concerns. We see the average individual, at his worst and in volume.

This unique opportunity helped me to learn a great deal about people in general. I now know, for instance, that regular people don't typically do irregular things because they are immoral, criminal, or stupid. I have discovered, instead, that people most often get into trouble because they lose sight of the 800-pound invisible gorilla. Problems arise when we, the general public, fail to keep our emotions in full view.

Most people are not, I have realized, emotionally well-practiced. We tend to misunderstand our fears and misinterpret our desires. We act when we ought to sit still; we *feel* when we should instead *think*, and in the end, this allows our emotions to handle us as opposed to us handling them.

Worse yet—though we are quick to rush into treatment, rehabilitation, or analysis when our emotional boats begin to sink—the ongoing, everyday preparation we receive for living our emotional lives tends to be very haphazard. While we're anxious to acknowledge how we feel these days, that seems to be about all we are willing to do. Instead of trying to adjust how we feel, so we can do something that (at least) resembles the right thing, we act upon the emotion at hand as if we have no other choice.

This got me thinking.

If my mother's way of doing business could rescue someone as emotionally mismanaged as me, could her know-how help others who make more minor emotional mistakes? Could my mother's wisdom somehow be boiled down, clarified, and passed on in some useful form?

Eventually, I realized that the answer to this question was yes. I found, in fact, that my mother's wisdoms, massaged and reworded, authored all of my best moments on the bench.

I have been the recipient of some very expensive education, and I have worked in some well-reputed law firms. But every time some defendant before me finally hung his head and said, "I see," it wasn't because of something I learned in my psychology, philosophy, or criminology classes. Neither my judicial courses nor my oratorical skills ever helped me convince any of them of a thing. I met my rare light bulb moments when I was able to rephrase and convey to these defendants something my mother had once told me. As a result, I began to wonder if she did not have lessons for us all.

Given the way that emotional meltdowns have become a regular feature of our society, from parents killing each other at hockey games to every known "rage" in the book, I contend that people's lack of emotional know-how has become an urgent concern. In a day and age when cutting someone off on the road can get you killed, I say that teaching people the deliberate and purposeful development of emotional skills is as important as teaching them to read. That's why I wrote *My Mother's Rules*. It is your textbook for this new learning endeavor. My aim was to digest and simplify the way my mother thinks and capture her mindset in the form of rules that will help you—as they helped me—learn how to cultivate what my mother does so well.

The underlying principle of all the rules is simply this. While you may have the right to feel the way you do, you may not realize that you also have the ability to feel just about any way you want. There is nothing you have more control over than yourself; your emotions are one of the few arenas in which you can dictate terms. They belong to you entirely, and while the rest of the world can affect them, you are still the one who will ultimately determine what they will be. In short, my mother's rules are about the proper emotion: what it is and how to find it. If you obey these rules, you will be better at thinking your way through how you feel.

But I don't want you to take my word for it. I intend to offer proof. Not the kind you're used to, maybe, but proof nevertheless. You see, I don't always trust experts or studies. I am leery of statistics. I think all of those things are subject to misuse and misinterpretation. While I find a bunch of letters strung behind some guy's name comforting when I am trying to pick a surgeon, it isn't nearly as soothing to me when I'm looking for advice on how to live. Frankly, I'd like to know how other people live their lives before I let them tell me how to live mine. I mean, think about it. If someone stays in school long enough, he will get a degree. But does this really mean he is perceptive, self-controlled, capable of wisdom? Personally, I know more than a few mental health professionals I wouldn't trust to help me change a light bulb. Besides, as a lawyer, I learned long ago that you can always find an expert willing to give just about any opinion you're looking to sell. More alarming yet is the fact that opposing counsel will find another expert just as qualified who will say exactly the opposite thing.

No, the proof I intend to offer is of a more substantial kind. I am going to tell you as much as possible about the woman whose rules I hope you'll follow. I believe her life, and the life she led me to, are the best evidence of what these rules can do. Besides, since they don't give out PhDs in common sense, what else can I do?

Here's how this thing is going to work. In the first half of the book, I'm going to tell you the stories of her life and mine broken down into chapters, and at the end of each chapter I'll spell out the rules used in the stories I just told. In the second half of the book, I'll tell you how I used those rules to untangle other people's lives while I was sitting on the bench. More rules, refined and amplified, will conclude those chapters as well.

I would, however, like to issue a warning about this book. Though my mother used these rules to handle some rather extreme situations, they are not intended as advice on dealing with the truly dangerous, lethal, or insane. They will not get you out of an abusive situation, save you from depression, or find you the perfect mate. If you are about to go under for the third time, you ought to find someone whose job it is to fix that sort of thing. My distrust of experts notwithstanding, sometimes the best and bravest thing to do is raise your hand and holler for help. I believe in therapy and medication when the appropriate circumstances present. I have had an opportunity to benefit from both, and I would never bash anyone else who did.

These rules, instead, are for your average individual who would like to develop a greater immunity to the ups and downs of life. They are for the regular guy who wants to stay level in an off-kilter world. In short, these rules are designed to help you develop what I call "cockpit cool," a state of mind that will serve you well no matter what the world has in store for you.

Cockpit cool is that airline pilot personality. You know, the one you can't really appreciate until you hear it in one of those situations where only the Black Box survives. These guys are working, talking, and never raising their voices right up until the end. Trained to keep their emotions in check, their rational brains work unencumbered until, well ... you know.

My mother displays that kind of cockpit cool right here on terra firma, and if you follow these rules you'll be able to do the same.

THE RULES

The Underlying Principles

You have to *work* at becoming a better emotional manager. But to start, you must first believe that you can control how you feel. Then, you have to make a point of doing so.

RULE NUMBER 1: The Smith and Wesson Test

Most people say that they can't help the way they feel. This is neither good nor true.

"I can't ... " is a powerful phrase that is very often misused. Typically, when we say "I can't," it isn't the literal truth. A man having a seizure or a woman giving birth truly *can't* stop. But most of the time when people say "I can't," they really mean "it's hard," "I don't want to," or "I'd really rather not ... "

This is especially true when we talk about changing how we feel.

In order to be a good emotional manager, you must decide that you have the ability to choose how you want to feel, and the best way to do that is to take the Smith and Wesson test. Ask yourself, "If someone put a gun to my head, would I be able to stop screaming at my kids?" If the answer to that question is "yes," then your problem is not so much about ability as it is a matter of motivation.

Case in Point: Once, in a church down south, the story goes, Martin Luther King Jr. was addressing a group of protesters. Things had gotten ugly outside what with all of the dogs and hoses and such. When he spoke that day, he said something very simple, but it was most important. He said, "The first thing we must do is *decide* not to panic." This is exactly what I'm talking about.

RULE NUMBER 2: Work Your Emotions Like a Job

Practice. You have to address how you feel through what you do and the way you look at things. You have to work your emotions like a job. You must address them specifically, deciding that you will *make* your emotions follow your actions and not the other way around. Don't wait to change unproductive behavior until you *feel* like doing something else—you have to do the right thing when it feels all wrong. Keep doing it no matter what. Then slowly but surely what you feel will start to follow what you do.

Case in Point: My mother and I go into this kind of emotional training all of the time. If a certain feeling is not serving us well, we put new procedures into place to address our errant emotions. For instance, my mother, when she was newly widowed, had gotten a bad case of the sads. She was doing a whole lot of nothing all day long and it was making her depressed. She realized at one point that all the nothing started by watching TV. She'd turn on the set first thing in the morning and lay in bed watching it all day.

So one day she took the TV and turned it around to the wall. When I asked her why, she said, "I'm training myself not to watch it. That way I force myself to find something to do, which keeps me from lying around. And if I don't lie around I feel better."

Two

Education

Though known for giving long-winded advice, Toni Toler tends to tell very short personal stories. Having little room in her emotional house for reminiscence or regret, my mother doesn't see the point in looking back all that much. As a result, I had a hard time fleshing out the details of her early life. Whenever I asked her about them, she was intentionally vague. Alternately claiming loss of memory and simple ignorance, she contends it's all a blur.

Compounding the problem is my mother's belief that it's okay to tell a lie or two, if your purpose is a good one. Accordingly, my mother lies, both often and well, if she feels the truth will get in someone's way.

These difficulties notwithstanding, I have managed to piece together a reasonably accurate story. I pestered her when I thought it would do some good—like when she was angling for an invitation to come up and see her grandchildren. I asked my sister for a lot of information too, and I contacted a few of my father's friends. And last, but certainly by no means least, I read a diary my mother kept for a whole five days in 1965.

My mother's tale starts in Kansas City, where a thirteen-year-old girl named Sally married a man named Lee. These were my grandparents. Less than a year later, Grandma Sally gave birth to her first child, Lee Jr. Soon thereafter, she had Shirley, who most people now call Toni and who my sister, Kathy, and I call Mom. Next, Sally gave birth to a set of twins, Leatrice and Loreatha Jean.

My grandfather, Lee, was a chef, and a rather good one, I understand. Unfortunately, however, he was also quite an accomplished drinker. The chef thing made him a good provider. The drinking just made him mean, and since Sally was no shrinking violet, things occasionally got out of hand. Until the day she died, Sally was unable to bend the index finger of her right hand, after its tendons were cut in a knife fight with my grandfather. The kids used to get involved as well when Sally needed their support. They got together once, when Mom was only five- or six-years-old, and took a hammer to their father's toes.

Given the volatile nature of my grandparents' relationship, I'm not really sure how upset everyone was when my grandfather up and walked off one day. My mother and her siblings were still very young, and I imagine that, on some level, they must have enjoyed the calm his departure brought. But peace and quiet notwithstanding, there was still the matter of money. An absent husband left young Sally with nothing but a sixth-grade education and four small children to support. At some point, she landed a job in a hairpin factory, but I'm not sure when that happened. I do know, however, that on at least one occasion, Sally was required to put her kids into an orphanage because she could not afford to feed them.

I make special note of the orphanage because it is one of the few stories my mother has told me voluntarily and in detail. "It was a tough place to be," she said. "The ladies would beat our heads against the sink when they washed out the ringworm medicine my mother used to put in our hair," because they were angered by the mess it made on the pillows.

But that wasn't the worst of it for Mom. She felt imprisoned there. She spent an awful lot of time looking beyond the fence at all of the places she could not go. She wanted to be like the little girl she saw who played in the backyard of the house next door. Mom thought that little girl had everything that she could ever desire: a backyard, nice dresses, parents, and a house of her very own. "If I could only get out and play with her," Mom thought, "everything would be okay."

So, when my Sally came to get my mother and her siblings from the orphanage, Mom broke for the gate and made a beeline for that little girl's back yard. "I was so excited," Mom said, "that I ran over to her with arms outstretched yelling 'Little girl, little girl!'" Not knowing quite what to make of my aggressively advancing mother, that little girl screamed and ran away.

Now here's the important part. Mom said that when that little girl ran away, she stopped and looked around. Realizing then that the little girl was also poor and didn't have all of the things that Mom imagined, Mom decided, "It's not so great out here," shrugged her shoulders, and walked back to Sally.

She told me that she got mad at herself for having spent all of that time longing for something that wasn't real. Her want, she concluded, had been misplaced. Her longing, it seemed, had been wasted. "I decided then and there," my mother said, "that I'd never do that to myself again. I was never going to let how I feel make something bad feel even worse."

Of course, if I were you, I probably would not believe this story; it sounds too Hollywood. How many nine-year-olds do you know who could come up with this sort of thing? But if you hang on for a few more chapters I believe I can convince you that it's true. This theme repeats itself often in my mother's life.

Now, since this isn't a fairy tale, my mother's revelation and rescue from the orphanage was not the beginning of a new and better life. As I'll address later, some bad things end just so you know how much worse things can get. Young, uneducated, and under pressure, my grandmother, it appears, had a little trouble with the parenting thing. Not knowing how else to raise her kids, she routinely beat them with electrical cords and broomsticks. And if they moved too much while being whipped, they got tied to the bed. In fact, my mother thinks that her brother, Lee, was not born with the intellectual difficulties from which he suffered, but rather came by them as a result of all the stuff Sally broke over his head.

They lived in crowded circumstances, in unpleasant and unsafe neighborhoods. They moved in and out of relatives' homes. They never had anything that one could identify as new. Just getting by, an often-angry Sally would remind them that, "If it wasn't for you, I could be laid up with some man."

Here, my story fails a bit due to my mother's unwillingness to fill it out. Convinced that all of us have some unpleasantness lurking in their history, my mother "sees no point in comparing pain," as she puts it. She does, however, admit to one momentarily compelling emotional need. "For the longest," she once told me, "I couldn't understand how our father could allow us to be so desperately poor. I wanted to talk to him," she said, "and tell him how things were. I thought if he only knew how bad things had gotten, he'd come back to help."

So when she was 17, my mother found out where Lee was; a close relative ratted him out. He had returned to St. Louis, where he had family. Mom says she pestered the living daylights out of Sally for a chance to go and see him. "We really didn't have the money for that kind of thing," Mom said, "but my mother got the money together somehow. I'll always be grateful for that." Despite the issues my mother had with Sally, she always gave her mother her due.

When Mom got to St. Louis, Lee was nice to her and even gave her six dollars. "But he asked for it back two days later because he needed whiskey money," Mom added. My mother claims that this event solved the mystery for her, and put her sense of abandonment to bed. "This man is an alcoholic," she realized. "Whiskey tells him what to do." Satisfied with this explanation, Mom got on a bus and went home.

"Weren't you upset that you weren't any more important to him?" I asked, refusing to believe she was really so zen about the whole thing.

"When I was young," she said, "I didn't really understand what alcohol could do to a person. But by the time I went to see him in St. Louis, I had seen enough to know that when liquor gets you, it gets you. None of the drunks around where I lived treated their families well. What would make him any different? You can't take it personally."

And that, I believe, in a nutshell, is what is so extraordinary about Mom. She has an innate ability to understand the emotional implications of any situation. I think that's what allowed my mother to avoid the things that being young and poor so often creates. Unlike so many who crumble under the pressure, my mother managed to separate herself emotionally from the circumstances in which she lived. She says she found refuge in the written word. My mother told me on more than one occasion, "books saved my life." They were what she took up—instead of drugs or men. Books were what she used to feel okay at times when life said she should not. No man, no drug, no amount of fun was better than the worlds she went to in books.

There is not much more detail I can give you about Mom in her teenage years. She'll smile and say she doesn't remember them, even though I know she does. All I know is that at eighteen, my mother left for junior college in Detroit, something I never quite understood and have repeatedly asked her about.

"So whose idea was that?" I asked, while trying to complete this chapter. And here, again, she claims that age and time have stolen that information. She does know it wasn't her mother's idea. Sally expressed no interest in schooling. "She had no frame of reference," my Mom explains. "You have got to remember that she only had a sixth-grade education."

Upon my mother's departure to junior college, Sally gave her thirty dollars, her sincere best wishes, and the distinct impression that Mom was not to return. Still very much a poor girl when she got to Wayne State, Mom went to school during the day, worked in a Ford factory at night, and moonlighted at a flower shop on the weekends.

Again, this part of her life is sketchy. Admitting that factory work was difficult, she said she just tried to focus on the cash. At Ford, she made more money than young, black, and uneducated typically allowed. "But I made it a point not to be satisfied with that," she said. She laid her bets on junior college. "I had no idea where I was going, but I knew I wasn't supposed to stop there."

My mother worked and went to school for two years until two unrelated events combined to redirect her life. She got laid off from the Ford factory, and Della Reese came into town. Mom's friend Mary wanted to go see Della sing. Typically, my mother would have told Mary no. She hated bars and drinkers. In fact, she didn't like to go out much at all. "If it wasn't on the direct path to not being poor," Mom told me, "I had no use for it." But since Mom had recently been laid off, she had lost her best excuse for not having a social life. So Mary convinced her and off they went. Mom now believes it was an act of God.

Mary and Mom never got to see Della Reese. They were thrown out of the club where she was appearing because they wouldn't buy any drinks. Interpreting their unceremonious dismissal as a sign that they ought to go home, my mother had to be pushed into going to another bar around the corner. It was crowded and they had to share a table with two men who were already there, one of whom was a big red-headed guy named Alex from Columbus, Ohio.

Alex was in Detroit to attend an NAACP conference. More importantly, he was the best friend of the man who would eventually become my father. His friend, Bill Toler (aka Daddy), had just gotten a divorce. Alex wholeheartedly believed that my father was the kind of guy who really needed a wife. They were good friends, the fiercely loyal, loud, and boisterous type. They did things for one another, which included, as my mother soon found, grand gestures of all kinds.

Fully aware that Daddy was a good man with some rather outstanding idiosyncrasies, Alex knew that my father needed a strong, solid, serious woman to stabilize his boat and for some reason, during the time they shared the table in that bar, Alex became convinced that my mother was just that woman. How or why neither my mother nor I have a clue. She was beautiful, no doubt, which is always a plus, but I think he liked her quiet soulfulness, her refusal to flirt, be forward or be coy. I call it Mom's inherently reserved nature. She says she was just backward and shy. Whatever the reason, Alex was so confident in his conclusion that he said he'd pay for her to come to Columbus and meet my father.

When my mother (sensibly) refused his offer, he said he would buy tickets for both my mother and Mary to come to Columbus and put them both up in a hotel. Emboldened by the promised presence of her friend, my mother reluctantly said yes.

So Mom went, with Mary in tow, and apparently my parents hit it off. They were married five months later. The speed of their courtship notwithstanding, they had a bumpy road to the altar. In those short five months between the time they met and when they finally said "I do," my father managed to stand my mother up twice. The first time, Daddy drove to Detroit to pick her up. From there they were going to travel to Chicago to get married. He got to Detroit okay, but on the way to Chicago, he started to sweat. As Chi-town neared, the problem got worse. By the time they got there Daddy was soaked from top to bottom, and it was clear that Daddy wasn't going to make it. He apologized, quite sincerely, Mom said, then turned around and drove her home.

Thirty days later, they decided to give it another try. Plans, however, were simplified. All Daddy was supposed to do this time was get to Detroit and meet her at city hall. I guess he figured the less time he had to think about it, the more likely it was he'd get through it.

My mother arrived at the agreed-upon destination, but he neither came nor called. When she finally got a hold of him some three or four days later, Daddy simply said that he had gotten tied up. Years later, she learned that this lame explanation was almost the literal truth. Daddy had gotten drunk and into a fight the night before, and at the time of their scheduled nuptials, he was stuck in jail.

Weeks later they tried again. Reasoning, I assume, that his travel plans were the problem, this time he suggested that she come to him. My mother recalls his exact words. "You can come on now, I'm ready." If you ask me, it sounds a little like a man submitting to his executioner's noose. But who am I to criticize? Remarkably, Mom gave up her apartment, sold all her furniture, and moved to Columbus. Luckily, however, this time Daddy actually managed to say, "I do."

Now, to tell you the truth, I believe that if my mother had known just how much trouble he was going to be, she may not have done it. Being the rational woman that she was, I think she would have run. But she was young and she believed in herself. She knew how strong she was and had not yet fully honed her Second Set of Eyes (about which you'll learn more later). So—despite even some dire predictions from the people who knew my father the best—she took him on. Deliberately picking her poison, she left the devil of poverty for the dark prince of the unknown.

"Why?" I asked, while writing this chapter. The decision never made much sense to me. My mother, however, is very clear on this one particular point in her past. It wasn't a mad, head-over-heels love thing. Nor did either of my parents believe they had found their soul mate. Instead, both of my parents made a conscious decision about who they were going to love.

Mom and Dad were both deliberate people who wanted the very same things. Long before mom had begun working her way out of Chicago's South Side, Daddy had been working his way out of abject poverty and the coal mines of West Virginia. He had joined the army, fought in a war, and went to law school on the GI Bill. By the time he had met my mother, he was in the midst of a very successful law practice. He looked at most things just like she did. They both believed that their futures were up to them, no matter the nature of the obstacles. They both knew and respected hard work. They were both headed in the same direction.

Despite their similarities, they each had something the other needed. He had to have stability and she knew she could provide it. Mom, on the other hand, wanted a middle-class existence, and that my father could give her. More importantly, each saw that the other had a value system that matched. Dad was a good man, a guy true to his word, well respected by everyone who knew him, and Mom was quite old fashioned in a Fifties kind of way. She believed in the good-wife, picket-fence thing, even though black and ghetto-born suggested that she should not. Add that to a mutual desire for children and you have several good reasons for both of them to say "I do."

Of course, you already know that my mom and dad did not end up living an Ozzie and Harriet existence. And being a realistic woman, Mom knew that that wasn't really in the cards. She had seen all of the warning signs. She saw him intoxicated and out of control on several occasions while they were dating. A number of his friends even told her not to do it because he was out of his mind. But she was tough, and she knew it. She had seen quite a bit in life already and managed to get through it just fine. She simply thought she could handle him, pull him together, and rein him in. After all, I suppose she thought, "How much trouble could one 5'2", 135-pound man be?

So they got married and once they did, Daddy moved her into the house he had built at 1187 South Weyant, which as far as I'm concerned, is where all of the trouble started.

THE RULES

The Codification of Attitude and Outlook

I have made my mother tell me the orphanage story over and over again. I want to know how she pulled such a rational idea out of a purely emotional situation, especially at an age where rational usually has yet to develop in full form.

Unable to come up with any other explanation, I have decided that Mom was blessed from the very beginning with what she calls her Second Set of Eyes. Her Second Set of Eyes is the name she has given to her ability to see past herself. They are what she uses to watch the rest of the world without interference from her own emotional static.

While my own Second Set of Eyes is not quite as good as Mom's, it has served me well. This next set of rules is designed to help you create your own. It is a difficult but doable process that has several steps. The first step requires you to figure out just who you are. You need to know just what's wrong with the eyes you have before you learn to create new ones.

The second step requires you to choose how you want to see the world. It asks you to make a conscious decision about what your emotional outlook will be.

RULE NUMBER 3: The Bathroom Mirror Mandate

There are all kinds of people in this world, and as much as we would like to think of ourselves as wholly different and unique, in a world full of snobs, jerks, and geniuses—of pests and partiers—of the sad, the stupid, and the simply off their rocker—of the kind and the weak, the driven and the giving—odds are that you, too, are sporting an identifiable personality quirk that may not be serving you well.

This rule asks you to stare deep into the eyes of your lesser self to find your weaknesses. It requires you to take a good hard look inside. It asks you to fight the urge to put your best foot forward and focus on the one that's dragging behind.

In order to comply with this rule you must think through all of your major mistakes. Search out their causes, peruse them for patterns, and then figure out what they say about you. Reexamine the things other people say about you, not in order to determine whether they are right, but in an effort to understand how they came to their conclusion. Even if you are not who they say you are, you have to consider this: is what you're doing conveying something other than what you intend?

The point of all of this soul-searching is for you to gain a heightened state of awareness. Remember, your faults and weaknesses will never hurt anyone else as much as they'll hurt you. But if you know what they are and understand how they work, they will be much less likely to do you harm.

This rule also requires that you take into consideration all the stuff political correctness claims doesn't matter, but in fact really does. How you feel and what you think has a lot to do with your gender, race, class, education, and exposure. Your hormones have not read Gloria Steinem; nor has your upbringing been debriefed. Both will drive you to do things they are programmed to do, politically correct or not. You must accept that we are all human, and as such we *necessarily* harbor prejudices, ones that often rest so close to us they are almost impossible to see.

Case in Point: Here's exactly how it's done:

I talk too much, and I talk too fast, and if I'm talking to someone who I think talks too slowly, I'll finish his sentences for him. I tend to look for the worst in everything and the best in everybody. I bore quickly and spook even faster. I have been known to get distracted by my own thoughts. I engage in worry as an art form, and let the most mundane things unnerve me. Details can walk right by me and I'll never even see them. I have no domestic abilities, despite my ongoing and deliberate attempts to acquire them. I am a control freak and tend to suffer from all the fears and power absorption that this trait often inspires.

I know all of these things about myself, but never use them as excuses. I keep these monsters well in my sights whenever I enter a situation that will implicate one of them, because I know that the first battle in any war I fight is always going to be with me.

RULE NUMBER 4: The Rule of Inclusion

Most of us are not born on the south side of Chicago. Lots of us got better; some of us got worse. Likewise, most people don't live with someone (like my father) who sees breaking out windows as a reasonable response to burned biscuits. Be that as it may, we all have stuff to deal with. Big, small, or otherwise, everyone has some kind of misfortune.

This rule requires us to acknowledge, out loud, that there is nothing so special about any one of us that exempts us from misfortune. My mother's answer to the question "Why me?" is always "Why *not* you? Why should you get a free pass on all of that the pain and suffering the whole world has known since the beginning of time?"

Distress is all a part of it. No one has singled you out. And if you can ban the feeling of being unfairly targeted that often accompanies misfortune, you can remove an entire layer of emotional baggage that you really don't need.

Lack of fairness is not an excuse for bad behavior; it is simply information. If you are required to jump five hurdles to everyone else's three, and if you are unable to remove the extra ones, you are left with two options. You can remain at the starting line, ranting and raving in a fit of unproductive indignation. Or you can jump over those hurdles. Either way, the race will end when it ends. Where you're standing when it does, however, is completely up to you.

Case in Point: Typically, when I saw a young lady in court on an assault charge, it had to do with "his other baby's momma drama." That's when some woman who has a baby with a man gets upset because he's left her for some other woman with whom he also has a child. One day, Momma #1 sees Momma #2 and then the fight is on, because Momma #1 believes that if not for Momma #2 she would still have her man.

Of course, this is not the case at all. Momma #1's troubles started much earlier, when she chose to date a man who already had two kids by two other women he now ignores. You see, she believed him when he said "Baby, you're special," because that was what she wanted to hear. It felt right so she let it hide the logic of the situation. It helped explain away the trail of broken hearts and unsupported babies he had all over town.

The Rule of Inclusion does not allow you to think like that. It reminds you that as special as you are to yourself, the rest of the world doesn't see you that way. For Momma #1 in particular, it requires you to acknowledge that whatever he said to you, he probably said to those other women. After all, none of them would have had his baby if he had told them, "Yo, you're nothing but a good time until I find someone I truly love."

RULE NUMBER 5: No Matter What, Keep Coming

If I had a dime for every time my mother said "Keep coming," I would never have to work again. This rule is very simple. It says that absent willpower, all of the opportunity in the world doesn't mean a thing. In order to keep coming, you must decide that neither your situation nor the people around you can define who you are or determine what you can do.

Don't get me wrong. I'm not saying that you can do anything if you try. Sometimes, no matter what you do, there will be some things you can't overcome. But even if effort will not guarantee success, this rule requires you to acknowledge that its absence guarantees failure.

Case in Point: I was 33 when I ran for judge the first time, a young black woman in a predominantly white community. One of my opponents was a well-respected attorney who had lived in this city and practiced law twelve years longer than I had been alive. I belonged to a political party whose members were outnumbered, in my neighborhood, five to one. Solitary by nature, I didn't belong to a lot of organizations, and I could not tell you the names of the people who lived two houses down my street.

Everyone, and I mean everyone, told me I couldn't win. Even the guys who talked me into it said it couldn't be done. They just wanted me to get some experience so I would have a better chance the next time around. I wrapped my arms around all of the things people said were stacked against me and used them to my advantage. I hit the black parts of town hard, because most people said that the blacks were the least inclined to vote. I went to their houses two or three times, right before the election, reminding them what a unique opportunity they had. I went door to door for months. Young might not look very judicial, but it has very strong legs.

I worked twice as hard as the other candidates, pursuing the votes everyone else conceded, and much to the surprise of most (and to the alarm of some) I brought home a six-vote win.

RULE NUMBER 6: Get Amused

There are very few things in life that are not just a little bit funny. If you learn to get some pleasure out of your failings, the whole world will be easier to take.

One's sense of humor is invaluable when things aren't going well. It makes tolerable those terrible things you can neither change nor avoid. As hard as you may try, sometimes you just don't win. All of the effort in the world won't stop you from getting caught up in something that's completely beyond your control. Comics make careers out of searching for the absurdity in negative situations.

It is my contention that we would all be better off if we did the same thing. Getting amused is much more useful than getting frustrated, angry, or mad. The problem is you have to work on the first one, while the last three come naturally.

Case in Point: Despite the fact that I won my first election by only six votes, I got 80 percent of the votes when I ran for reelection. That achievement notwithstanding, I threw it all away on the heels of a telephone call from Hollywood and a job that lasted all of three months. My folly made all the local papers, making my state of unemployment the only thing anyone wanted to discuss with me for an entire year. Had I not been able to see how ridiculous my situation was, it could have become a problem when I had to discuss, with total strangers, seven to eight times a day, how it felt to make such a monumental mistake.

Three

Professional Experience:
Welcome Weyant Avenue

While it is easy to understand the beauty of my mother's escape from poverty, her decision to put up with my father is a bit more difficult to understand. In fact, there are those who would suggest that my mother's decision to stay was a terrible error she made over and over again.

Daddy was a handful—an all-day, every-day effort. He was, in fact, the kind of guy who got kicked out of the military for being too disruptive. According to one version of his army discharge story, my father pounced on white officers outside the officers' club when he realized that Negro trumped lieutenant and they wouldn't let him in. In another, he beat up a white enlisted man who refused to salute him because he was black.

Frankly, I'm not quite sure what happened; either story could be true. They both sound so much like him, and I knew better than to ask. In the end, however, the ins and outs of what he did are not important. What is important is the official reason the army gave for putting him out. "Psychosis" is the word his discharge papers used, also, "manic-depressive—manic type." These days they call it bipolar. Keep in mind, this happened in 1947.

I imagine that term, "psychosis," followed Daddy into the hospitals where he took his "rests" from time to time. It may even have been a word tossed around in reference to him among his friends. I know for sure that my mother used it while talking about him once I became an adult. But I knew nothing of the word, and what it meant, when it was affecting me the most.

Like all six-year-olds, I knew Daddy best for who he was in front of me. I was not acquainted with the able attorney his colleagues knew. The enormously principled man my mother married was not available to me either. The man I saw was the one he disassembled into when his day drew to a close. What I got was Daddy as he was winding down or starting to come apart.

Daddy, disassembled, came in two basic forms, and when I was small, Intoxicated was the one I saw the most. Mania is a tiresome thing that will not let you rest. Liquor was Daddy's sedative, the thing that let him go to bed. Jack Daniel's and Johnnie Walker made a very effective team. Together, they knew how to turn off all the relevant parts of his brain. Unfortunately, however, The Distilled Duo was as mischievous as it was able; they loved to arouse and agitate Pop before they nestled him off to sleep.

Jack and Johnnie gave my father license to feel without restraint. Misinterpreting threats and magnifying upsets, they inflamed his greatest fears. They encouraged him to call me a moron when I was three and would not speak. The Duo convinced Daddy that Mom was having affairs. At seven, I began fielding inquiries about the men my mother supposedly saw.

Once they persuaded him that Mom had stolen ten dollars. That particular piece of misinformation got Mom chased all of the way down the street. There was no infraction, real or imagined, that three of them could not inflate to crisis proportions.

The Distilled Duo, however, were not all bad. Carrying Jack and Johnnie around made Daddy slow, off-kilter, confused. He could be contained while in his cups. Drunk, he could run neither fast nor far. Drunk, his anger was short-lived. Daddy was far scarier when he had a clearer head.

For years, Intoxicated was just about all I knew of him. It is my most common memory of Daddy until I was eight or nine. But as I got older, and my world expanded, I began seeing other things. Some days I got to see him sober, focused, hard-working. He was beautiful to watch, a brilliant man who knew his profession well.

Unfortunately, I rarely got to see that version of my father, because most often I saw him at home. There, in later years, I was introduced to a whole new version of Daddy in his most destructive state, Unhinged.

Like Intoxicated, Unhinged often found small things quite important. But Unhinged was much more focused and persistent; the agitation of Unhinged knew no bounds. So while neither version of Daddy had any sense of proportion, there was one important difference between them. Unhinged could not let anything go, ever; Unhinged had no concept of time.

Once, Mom said something about Russian oil production that Daddy didn't believe and he proceeded to tear up the house. He carried on for so long that my mother was forced to call a couple of his friends to come over and calm him down. Although one of those friends confirmed the truth of Mom's comment, by then it was far too late for logic. Pop had to be hospitalized that day. It took three men to take him in.

Unhinged made dirt a problem. It could keep him up all night. He'd have Mom cleaning and scrubbing at all hours to the rhythm of unending complaint. Once, Daddy became completely undone when Mom forgot to buy someone a present. I still remember him standing over her, screaming at the top of his lungs. He raged for over an hour and would not let her move the entire time. Eventually, that day, Mom was required to do the last thing she wanted to do. She hollered down the hall for her daughters to come. She needed an assist.

Mom knew that if Daddy wasn't too far gone, seeing his daughters might give him pause. So we came toddling down the hall to see what we could do. On this particular day we didn't cry. I remember that distinctly. Instead we talked and tugged and pulled at his pants until he tired enough to see us. Then, at our behest he reluctantly consented to a game of Ring Around the Rosie. This, my mother says, was my sister Kathy's idea. She and I both took one hand and made him walk in a circle, although he refused to sing. Once or twice he tensed up as if he was going to explode, but we kept his hands in ours and sang of ashes, while Mom slipped away.

On another occasion, while leaving for work, Dad realized that the window shades did not descend equidistantly all of the way around the house. He called my mother every five minutes for the rest of the day to express his discontent. Telephone terror was not an uncommon thing with Daddy. Once the excessive amount of water used on the lawn led to a full eight hours of perpetual dialing. Misplaced car keys, buying the wrong soap—these sorts of things did it for Daddy as well.

While the phone calls were annoying, they provided my mother with an unusual sense of comfort. She knew that as long as Daddy was dialing, he wasn't on his way home.

Fortunately for me, however, to this day I'm not privy to all of the details of Unhinged. Lots happened while he was in that state that my sister and I were never meant to know. Daddy tried hard to direct his anger away from his daughters, whom he adored. Mom, likewise, hid the worst from us as much as she possibly could. Even now my mother maintains a principled silence on the subject. Some of it, she simply says, cannot be understood.

Accordingly, my sister and I usually just saw the aftermath of Unhinged. Like the time I woke to find my mother climbing out of the backyard dog house, where she had spent the night. When I asked her what she was doing in there she simply replied, "It was cold." Another night, I was startled out of sleep by my mother banging on my bedroom window. Outside in her nightgown, ankle deep in snow, Mom made a request. "Get me my car keys and a coat," she said. I passed them out the window.

At one point, Mom's unexpected exits became so commonplace that she began keeping a second purse and a blanket in her car, and a set of keys stashed outside of the house. That way, once chased out of the house, she could get away without having to go back in. Sometimes she took my sister and me with her; other times she did not. It all depended on where everybody was positioned relative to my father and the nearest available exit.

And that was my existence for a decade or so. Daddy, Disassembled, was all I knew of him. Whether Intoxicated or Unhinged, his unpredictability was our only constant. A perpetual sense of confusion bound my sister, Mom, and me in ways that were invisible to most people who knew us. We told nary a soul. Daddy was a private affair that required the three of us to function as one—that is, until Disassembled would shift and all of the boundaries would change. My parents would suddenly align themselves against some danger even greater than the one with which we lived. People would start calling the house. Mom spoke in secretive whispers. Sometimes she would have to go and *get* him from somewhere. Once or twice I awoke in the middle of the night to find nobody there.

I did not learn the nature of these undefined emergencies until I was much older. They were nothing but funny old stories by the time they got to me. Told over the kitchen table as entertainment, they were the stuff that, in later years, helped cement us all back together. One such tale involved a house on fire. Another told of various opposing counsel Daddy decked in court. There is even one about a client thrown down stairs. This may have happened more than once. The stories also include women of ill repute calling the house and asking my mother to come and retrieve her man.

Daddy apparently got in and out of trouble with great aplomb. There would be a crisis and then it would get fixed. Then after awhile the tension would die down and the house would return to our peculiar brand of normal. Of course, my sister and I had no clue what happened and all we felt was the looming presence of those events. They were just another layer of Disassembled with which we learned to live. And that, in the end, turned out to be the biggest problem I had to live with growing up.

Anticipation was the bitch, the beast with which I did daily battle. The outbursts themselves were far easier to handle. They required action, and (though it wasn't much more than an illusion) the ability to respond resembled some kind of control. Wondering when the worst was going to happen was the most difficult thing I faced. The *prospect* of upheaval was what kept me tied up in knots.

Even when Daddy wasn't home I was unable to relax, because when I was young, I didn't really know what Not Home meant, so I was never sure just how long Not Home would last. Sometimes I would not see him for days; on some days he returned home from work early. Early evening arrivals were not so bad, but they were very rare. Very late arrivals usually meant Intoxicated, the way I saw him most. Midday returns were the worst, though—they usually meant Unhinged. When you saw him coming and you didn't know why, the best thing to do was hide.

As the years passed, though, I began to understand Not Home. More often than not, Not Home meant that Daddy was At the Office. At the Office was a good thing. It had a reassuring sound. By then I had seen At the Office for myself, and I understood that it was the one place most likely to hold him. Daddy liked it there.

I know for a fact that the office is where he went the day the hospital misplaced him. Having managed to flee the psychiatric ward before he'd been "adjusted," he was being sought by the hospital when they made a desperate call to Mom. "Are you afraid, Mrs. Toler?" Mom said they asked. She told them she was fine. Then she suggested he might be At the Office and that, indeed, was where he was.

I knew, however, that At the Office was not the only place that meant Not Home. There were other enigmatic hinterlands that kept my father too. In the Streets was one such place, an indeterminate somewhere else I did not understand. It had no stated purpose and, unlike At the Office, Mom never took us there. All I knew is that when Daddy was In the Streets, he did this thing Mom called Run Amok.

Other times Not Home meant that he was Out of Town which, in and of itself, meant several different things. It could mean he was in another city, or in the hospital "resting." Or Out of Town could simply mean whereabouts unknown. All I knew about Out of Town was that it meant an extended stay, and that unlike At the Office it meant he might eventually show up back home in the middle of the day.

But like I said, more often than not Daddy was At the Office. This meant that my sister and I did not have to worry in earnest until 9:00 P.M. Baths taken, hair braided, and tucked in our beds, all we could do was wait it out. Would he come home, and if so, when? How long would we have to wait? More importantly, once he did get home, how Disassembled would he be?

Headlight beams dragging across the bedroom wall was how we knew Not Home was over. Our room abutted the driveway, so we always knew when he pulled up. Once we saw the light sweep past we'd lay still and listen, wondering whether the silence would yield to the distinctive sounds of discontent.

Most nights nothing happened at all. We might hear a door close and a mumble or two, but then the quiet would return. The sound of his arrival would melt into nothing and we'd fall back asleep.

Once or twice a month, however, things did not work out so well, and the ordinary sound of his return escalated into unrest. It was almost always the same. First a slamming door, then a strident rumbling that would burst into a "Goddamn it!" That was my father's go phrase, the evening's starting gun. Those nights I sat poised to intervene, waiting to see if Mom would call my name.

It wasn't always like that, though. Some days there was no build up, and the evening's drama would announce itself from the drive. Voices, loud and laughing, would herald the party he'd brought home with him. Hard-working and equally hard-drinking black men would accompany him into the house. Drunk when they arrived, they continued to drink once there, and sometimes fights broke out.

All these years later, I see these evenings as a diffuse whole instead of as distinct events. In fact, I own few isolated memories of anything that occurred. Things disassembled so often it all folds into one for me. What I recall is a collage of things that reoccurred and how they made me feel.

For instance, I remember my sister and me jumping the rose bushes that lined either side of our driveway. Well-tended and tall, there were not easy to clear. I took pride in my ability to hurdle them. I also register relief when I think about them because they were the last obstacle to safety.

I recall the Howard Johnson's East as a local motel we used to go to when home became too hot. The name, the sign, and the small, rectangular office all live in my head. Both comforting and disturbing, my images of Howard Johnson's East remind me of bad nights that had come to an end.

I also recall the local drive-in movie theaters as another frequent refuge. I remember liking both the hot dogs and sleeping in the car. Unresolved, however, is the most prominent emotion that image brings to mind. The drive-in never ended things; it was just a stop along the way. We'd have to go home when the second movie was over and, once there, I had a job to do.

Mom would wake my sister and me and take us to the back of the house. Then she'd put me up on her shoulders so I could look inside her bedroom window.

"Is he there?" she'd ask, "Is he asleep?" I'd look in to see where he was.

If the answer to both of these questions was 'yes,' we went in. But if I didn't see him, or if he was there and awake, we'd get back in the car and find someplace else to go.

One memory I hold is of a short green dress with a huge white pilgrim-like collar. I remember it only because I was momentarily struck by how ugly it was. Not knowing whether my father had yet to recover from the previous evening's Disassembly, we went from Howard Johnson's East directly to a bargain department store. Once there, Mom bought us new clothes—underwear, socks, shoes, and much to my dismay, that godawful green dress. We had to wash up in the store bathroom and then went straight to school.

I also own a picture of Mom holding me up to the living room window, waving me around like a flag. I had on a red skirt and patent leather shoes, and I was screaming bloody murder. Daddy was trying to break out a window so he could get in the house. Mom had locked him out because he was drunk and in a rage. I was the prop Mom used to get him to change his mind. "See what you're doing to the baby?" she said as held me to the window.

I also have a distinct memory of getting our ears pierced. Mom had done so with out my father's consent and Daddy didn't like it. Keloids, I later learned, were what made Daddy lose his mind that day. Some blacks have a tendency toward excessive scar tissue on injured skin. As a result, small injuries can grow large tumor-like growths—keloids—that can't be cut away without inviting more of the same.

Since Daddy could leap from incident to catastrophe in the blink of an eye, he saw pierced ears, went directly to keloids, and in due course after Mom. With the image of large baseball-like appendages hanging from our ears emblazoned across his mind, Daddy put Mom on the family room floor. I think she may have called my name, but I'm not sure about that. What I do recall is walking down the hall and seeing their struggling bodies framed in the family room doorway.

Momentarily distracted by the hysterical girl on his back, Daddy lost his grip and Mom wriggled loose. She took off down the hallway and flew out the front door. She then ran around to the Webster house next door and disappeared into their back yard.

I was fourteen when the light socket thing happened. Somehow my mother had done something that caused my father to conclude that she had somehow misused our lighting fixtures. He responded by getting a hammer and began to tear the light switches out of the walls. He was in his underwear—nylon, ecru-colored boxer shorts—and nothing else. His mouth was deeply inclined to one side. That was my father's tell, as the poker players call it. One side of his mouth would droop when he was drunk, the angle of its decline an accurate indicator of his intoxication level.

My mother, sister, and I beat a hasty retreat, but since he seemed pacified by his re-wiring efforts, we didn't run far. Eventually ending up on the back porch, my sister and I sat on either side of Mom, who was still holding the laundry she had been doing when things went bad.

Despite the suddenly flammable nature of our existence, our family still established routines and rituals. There was an odd order to the madness borne out of repetition, soothing if only for the sense of predictability it brought. And, of course, as time went on and I got older, the unpredictability began to fall away. By age ten, I knew that no matter how far gone he was, he'd never hurt my sister or me. Daddy would blow and bluster all around us, but we always remained safely in the eye of his storm. He did not, would not, could not, hurt us. We could rely on that. I also learned more about Not Home and how to gauge the length of his absences. I began to understand the difference between Out of Town and At the Office, and that, too, served to ease the angst.

But more important than all of this, I figured out that I could talk to Daddy when no one else could. We had an odd empathy, he and I. I often understood what he was thinking. While even I could not approach Unhinged, Intoxicated I could calm. From age five on I would take all of the words then available to me and use them to point Daddy toward bed. An odd state of composure for a child so typically scattered—calm and controlled, well-reasoned and logical—would fall over me like a blanket. At those moments I was able to speak a language his better self could hear even while the Distilled Duo were mumbling in his ear. And I could get him to *stop*; sometimes, not always, but often enough to give me a sense that I could keep the worst from happening one day at a time.

That was my very first hit of my favorite drug, control. I have yet to kick the habit. But at least now I know it's me, and not the world, that I must learn to command.

THE RULES

The Rules Related to Cool

As I wrote before, my mother has something I call Cockpit Cool. Cockpit Cool is not, however, something you are, but rather a process you engage in. Cockpit cool requires a heightened state of awareness and a willingness to adjust. This rule requires you to acknowledge that emotional management is always job number one. How you feel is always the first thing that you deal with before you deal with anything else.

RULE NUMBER: 7: Identify the Dog That's Barking

Don't just feel something and keep moving. Stop and give it a name. You cannot be in control of something if you don't know what it is. So at any given time, on any given day, you should be willing to, *and in fact make a habit of,* asking yourself the following question:

What am I feeling and why?

In order to get into the habit of it, you must train yourself. (See Rule Number 2, Work Your Emotions Like a Job). For instance, you can decide to do it at predetermined hours, or whenever you pass a mirror. But whatever you do, be faithful to it: this is an important task. Just feel it, name it—actually say what it is—then identify its source. Example: "I'm a little cranky ... the kids have been a handful this morning." Or, "Traffic was a bear today, I'm a little out of sorts."

Identifying the dog that's barking will help you keep from passing the wrong emotion around. By naming the source of your dismay, you can isolate it better. It will help you realize that it was the kids and the traffic that made you angry, and not what your boss just said. That way you're less likely to cuss out the wrong person in the wrong situation and add to the troubles you already have.

Case in Point: On occasion every judge has to do what one judge friend of mine calls "the acid rain dance." Some people need a good dressing down in order to keep from acting up. In a municipal court, we often see sixty cases in one day, one right after another. Those waiting to be called sit in the audience and watch all of the cases called before theirs.

The last thing any defendant wants to see is you yelling at the guy in front of him. No one wants to appear before a recently pissed-off judge. So, whenever I was required to do the acid rain dance, I always said to the next guy up, "Don't worry, I was just upset with him, it has nothing to do with you." That way he gets reassured and, more importantly, it gives me a chance to compartmentalize and adjust. It makes me acknowledge who upset me and keeps me from passing my irritation along.

RULE NUMBER 8: Then Meet Fido at the Door

A shifting mood always announces itself. You just have to learn to listen. If you're really in touch with your feelings, you can hear them howling long before they reach your door. Again, it just takes practice. You have to review your day when it's done. Ask yourself, "What really happened when I got mad at John?" "What was the first sign that I was about to explode?" Was a flushed face your clue that angry was home, or was your racing heart the first one up the drive? Did sad declare itself with words or with certain hours spent moping in the house?

After a while you'll start noticing shifts in mood without making the effort to do so. You'll see Fido walking up the drive and know just how big he is.

Case in Point: Once, while I was on the bench, a young Muslim man told me that he should not have to pay a traffic ticket because he was guided by the laws of God and not the laws of man. His claim aggravated me in a most uncharacteristic way. I was becoming angry. I could feel it right behind my ears.

I knew I was overreacting, though, because I am familiar with that burn. Realizing that I had no legitimate use for the fight-or-flight chemicals that were coursing through my veins, I froze for a moment, looked down at my hands, and told myself to stop. Since it became clear in that moment that something unidentified was going on with *me,* I swallowed my initial reaction and made a point of treating him like everyone else.

Then, when court was over, I sat down to source my anger. 9/11 hadn't happened yet, so there were no current world events that could have caused such ire. Moreover, many a Christian had come into my court and claimed, in essence, the devil made him do it, but I never got as annoyed with them as I was with this young man. So I continued to think and concentrated on my own little world to find the problem. And in due course I ran into my oldest stepson and one of my sister's childhood friends.

The stepson part was easy. He was sixteen at that time, and as teenagers are prone to believe, he thought he knew everything. Unemployed, out of school, in my house, and eating at my table, his conversion to Islam struck me as just another ploy to complain about the food. He was foolish then, but he's not so much anymore. In fact, he is now one of my favorite people, and I love him with all my heart. But at the time he was just an irritant and that's about all I could see.

Thankfully, however, I found that he, alone, was not enough to color my emotional landscape. Upon further consideration, I recalled my sister's childhood friend who married a man who claimed to be a Muslim. One day, he and I had a long discussion in which he tried to convince me that my religion was simply wrong. He also had a whole lot to say about men being the masters of their homes.

About a year later, he beat his wife, my sister's friend, to death. He then left her dead body with their three preschool-aged children in their apartment for several days until someone finally found them.

Of course, this man was not a good representative of Islam. Every religion, including my own, has, as Tony Brown once said, "a liberal sprinkling of fools." He just happened to be one of them. He was a thug and a bully who misused both his religion and his wife, the way so many thugs and bullies do. His behavior had nothing to do with Islam, its practices or its beliefs. My stepson's conversion to Islam, in fact, has done wonderful things for him. The important thing is that I took the time to find out where my response came from and as a result I was able to put a potential prejudice to bed. Though my rational self understood that you can't judge a whole religion based on one fool's conduct, my emotional self had yet to accept it. But since I keep a sharp eye out for new emotions, I was able to keep that one from affecting what I did.

By the way, I still keep a sharp eye out for that particular dog just to make sure it won't sneak up on me again. I never assume that I conquer anything completely. It is a mistake far too many people make.

RULE NUMBER 9: Get Your Mind Right

This simply means that once you realize that you are sporting an emotion that is not doing you any good, you must decide to feel differently. The trick is to pick a *specific* emotion that you believe will serve you better and consciously decide to adopt it.

Case in Point: I am a practical, direct individual who believes that the best way to get from point A to point B is, in fact, a straight line. As a result, bureaucracy in any form drives me to distraction. While waiting in line or filling out forms, my brain will leap all around the process, marveling at its lack of efficiency. This, in turn, will make me irritable and short with those in charge. That is, until one day Mom caught me about to lose my mind in line and said the following to me.

"Get your mind right," she said. "This process is what it is and there isn't a thing you can do about it. You should have been prepared when you came in here to feel a little annoyed and you should know enough not to pass it along. That woman up there didn't think up this mess and she has a job to do. All day long she deals with impatient people like you who are angry with her for something that is not her fault. If you want this thing to go a little smoother, go up there and be especially nice. Sympathize with the problems she has, and she'll be more likely to go out of her way for you. Either way, this process is what it is. How you feel when you leave this place is completely up to you."

RULE NUMBER 10: Learn to Act in Opposition to How You Feel

In order to get your mind right, you have to learn to act in opposition to how you feel. In order to do this, follow the steps below.

A. Give It Voice

This is a very powerful thing. "Tell yourself you can." Mom's said it a million times. "Talk yourself into it. Say it out loud, it's easier that way."

To give something voice requires you to put your feelings into words. And when I say give it voice, I mean exactly that. Don't just think it. Actually open up your mouth and make some noise. Or better yet, put it down on paper. When you say something out loud, or see it in writing, it helps put shape to an unformed idea, and once anything takes on concrete form, it's easier to handle.

You should give voice to all kinds of things. Anticipate, out loud, impending upset and how you would like to respond to it. Say, for instance, "This traffic jam has me all worked up, but I am not going to go into the office and spread this thing around."

Personality flaws and bad moods are great things to put into words. When your ten-year- old is acting up, say something like, "I am not going to let my bad mood decide how I talk to my kids this morning." Or "I am a grown woman and I am better than that." Then *tell* Junior that you love him. Let that be the next thing that you say. Emotions can really follow words. It will be much harder to smack the boy if you just told him that you loved him.

Case in Point: When I first started practicing law, a seasoned litigator told me that when you have a bad fact in a case, tell the jury about it up front, then ask each juror to promise you individually and *out loud* not to hold it against your client. He said that it had been his experience that when people have been made to promise like that, they are much more likely to do it.

Point in Action: Every morning my husband gets a weather report. I sit on the side of the bed, search my mood, then tell him how I feel. Happy, sad, energized, or angry, I give my husband the full 411.

Since I know I can be moody, I make extra-sure it doesn't get in my way. Giving voice to whatever mood I'm in puts it directly in my sights. That way it won't creep up on me without my knowing and start telling me what to do.

B. Always Have a Game Plan

If you have complied with Rule Number 3: The Bathroom Mirror Mandate, you should know what sets upsets you. So whenever you are scheduled to encounter one of your triggers, form a game plan to help you through it. There are lots of ways to do this and you can think up some on your own. But the following four are the ones I use. They may give you some ideas.

1. Walk around it. This is my favorite one. The easiest way to stay out of trouble is to stay away from where it lives. While I recognize that I have the right to go just about anywhere, I also acknowledge that there are certain places a person like me ought not be.

Case in Point: Take, for instance, this thing I have about Oreo Double-Stuf cookies. I can't stop eating them once I get them, and I can't pass by a package without buying it. Of course, this is a very good excuse to carry an extra twenty pounds around. So I learned just how far down the cookie aisle I can go with out catching a glimpse of that beautiful pink and white package.

2. Fight it out. Of course, you can't always avoid things. Sometimes you simply have to stand your ground and fight. But in doing so, you must remember that the first battle you must engage in is always with yourself. You have to give voice to any weakness that might be implicated in what you are about to face. Remind yourself what they are and what they tend to make you do. Then you must—again, out loud—tell yourself what you need to do.

Case in Point: I, for instance, do not like to drive somewhere I've never been before. Silly, I know, but what can I say? I'm still my Daddy's daughter. I do not, however, let that stop me. Instead, I fight it out. I stop worrying about which road to take or what the traffic will be like and focus on the real problem. "You better get in that car," is what I say to myself. "You're forty-some-odd-years-old. Are you going to let some silly fear tell you what to do?" Though I'm still a little uptight when I get in the car, I always end up going. Then that once-unfamiliar place becomes somewhere I know how to get.

3. Enlist assistance. Find somebody in your life who loves you and is not afraid to give you a little crap. Tell them what it is you need to do and ask them to help you do it. The trick to this rule is making the emotional adjustments necessary to handle this kind of help. You can't get mad at people for doing what you asked them to do, even if in the process of doing it, they manage to get on your nerves. So keep reminding yourself that you asked them to do this thing and that anything worth doing at all usually hurts a little.

Case in Point: When I ran for judge the first time, I had to go door to door. I had to walk up to household after household and talk to people I didn't know. This is not the kind of thing a person like me ever wants to do. I am naturally nervous, basically shy, and don't like to bother people. My husband, on the other hand, thought the whole thing sounded like grand fun. So I let him take charge of my walking schedule. He'd tell me where to go and just how many houses I'd have to hit. And though every once in a while we got into it because he was putting the pressure on, I knew enough not to get too angry and to do as I was told.

4. Take it to another level. When faced with something you don't want to do, pretend that it is something other than what it is. It does not have to be reasonable, nor does it need to make sense to anyone but you. It is simply a means to an end, a way to get you where you're going.

Case in Point: When I went campaigning door to door, I sometimes made it into a game. I'd make bets with myself as to whether someone was home or about the gender of the person answering the door. A silly thing, I do admit, but it kept me from thinking about the negative aspects of my task. Hundreds of doors later, I had lost five pounds and earned myself a new job.

▶ *Four*

Awards and Recognition

It could be argued, very convincingly, that Mom simply should have left. I can hear the experts now: Toni Toler stayed in an abusive relationship for all of the very same reasons women so often do: finances, fear, lack of self-esteem, a mistaken belief that she could "fix" her husband. Of course, I cannot blame those experts; after all they were not there. What's more, Mom's sounds like such a common story. I heard it often while on the bench.

In fact, had you asked me thirty years ago, I would have sided with the experts. I wanted off of Weyant Avenue in the worst way. I thought living anywhere would be better than living with Daddy.

Of course, I don't feel that way now. If I did, this would be a very different book. As it stands, I like the way the story turns out, rough days, bad nights, and all. I like who I am and I recognize that, at least in part, my upbringing made me this way.

Of course, anyone can look back, connect the dots, and say this decision led to that ending. But when you are in the middle of something you don't have that kind of help. My mother had no way of knowing how things would turn out. The objective facts at the time all indicated that her life with this man was a disaster in the making. So what was she thinking? How did she know that such a difficult situation would turn out all right? Was she clairvoyant, prescient, prophetic, or was it just dumb luck?

Once I started writing this book, I realized I needed an answer to those questions. Simply looking back, I soon realized, would not clear them up. I needed more information. So I called her, again. Not just for stories, this time, but for an explanation. I wanted to know *why* she did what she did. I wanted to know what she was thinking. Did she have a clear view of what could be, or was she just out of her mind?

"Lynnie," she said, "are you still writing that book?"

What else could I say but, "Yes, Mommy."

"What you need to do is get a real job and stop worrying about what went on thirty years ago."

My mother and I have had this conversation a number of times in the past couple of years. She does not see the beauty in what she did; she thinks this book is silly.

"Yeah, Mom, I know, but nevertheless, I need some information."

She sighed and asked me what I wanted because she knew it would be easier that way. Mom and I are very good at agreeing to disagree. Once we know where the other one stands (with no plans to move), we don't waste time getting mad. We simply work something out so both of us can move on.

"So why didn't you leave?" I asked again, having gotten the preliminaries out of the way.

"I *did* try to leave him once," she said, "but I decided that wasn't fair to you and your sister. Don't you remember when went to stay with Mother Dear?"

Mother Dear was what we called Sally, my grandmother, and yes indeed I remembered that visit. It was the long hot summer, the one we spent on the South Side of Chicago—6812 South Perry, I still remember the address.

"I thought we were just visiting." I say.

"No. I had left. But in the end I couldn't do it." Then she asked, with some level of incredulity, "Don't you remember how it was?"

Crowded and hot. That's all I remember. Mom had to fill in the rest, and this is what she told me. There were three adults and four children living in a one-bedroom third-floor walkup. It was ninety-five degrees every day, and all we had were a couple of fans. The Blackstone Rangers, the gang *du jour,* made going outside a problem, so we kids spent a lot of time in the house sweating up a storm. We couldn't get anywhere a bus couldn't take us, and waiting for a bus was an adventure in itself.

Kathy and I, my mother explained, were not used to this. We were children of comfort. Air conditioning, big cars, and cleaning ladies were what we knew of life. Deprivation was a new thing, Mom said, and we didn't like it at all.

Now, to be honest, I don't think I ever sat down and compared the relative miseries of my alternate hells: hot and poor on the South Side of Chicago versus running and hiding from Dad. At the time we stayed with Mother Dear, I was all of six years old and generally loopy, pretty much incapable of that kind of rational thought. But according to Mom, my sister, Kathy, had made that comparison, and she made up her mind. She much preferred the chaos of her comfortable home to the rocky peace of Chicago's impoverished South Side. Mom said that when Daddy called one night, Kathy got on the phone and told him, "Tell Mommy it's time to go home."

"That's when I knew," Mom said, "that I couldn't do this to the two of you. I had been poor and I could go back. I knew how to work and wasn't afraid of it. But you guys wouldn't have been happy." A pause then. "Besides, I knew your father would never hurt the two of you. And I knew that I was strong enough to make it work."

"But don't you think," I asked, "I would have been better off if I didn't have to live with Daddy?"

"Who knows?" she said, "It's not always about the *right* decision, Lynn. Sometimes it's just a matter of picking which set of problems you want to solve."

"So if you had it to do all over again, would you do the same thing?"

A chuckle. "I'm not sure. He *was* an awful lot of trouble." Another pause. "But he was a good man, Lynnie. You had better say that in your book."

And this, she later explained to me, was the main reason she believed that staying with Dad would work: "You can work with a good man that has bad habits because he wants to do the right thing. But a man with no character doesn't give a damn and you can't do anything with that."

So Mom went back with Kathy and me in tow, to deal with the problems she had purposely picked. And this is when she honed her Second Set of Eyes and perfected her emotional skills.

Now, I'm not claiming she fixed him. No one can cure psychosis by sheer force of will. What she did was manage her emotions so well that she could help him manage his. She couldn't stop the rollercoaster, but occasionally she was able to adjust its speed. She also kept herself from getting sick so she could keep an eye on everybody else. That way she could make sure that both of her daughters—even me, the one who wasn't strapped in too well—didn't fall off the ride.

As far as I can tell, my mother saw her first job as containment. She had to keep a lid on the chaos, which meant she had to control Daddy's environment as much as she could. Daddy was never fully present anywhere he was. His mind moved at a million miles an hour, and the rest of him never caught up. As a result, he lost things by the gross and couldn't find an object he had in his own hands. Not having something he wanted right away and couldn't find could send him into orbit, tearing up the house or tearing after Mom. So my mother bought things like reading glasses and spare sets of keys a dozen at a time. This would preclude any unnecessary meltdowns that might occur before she could get him out of the house.

Of course, getting him out was only half the battle. Eventually, he always came back home. Mom had to make sure the house was immaculate for whenever he got back from work. "Now, we could mess it up all we wanted once he got there," Mom says about Daddy's take on clean. "But initially he needed to be met with *pristine order*." Mom emphasizes the word "pristine" and says the word "order" with exaggerated authority whenever she tells this story. The chaos in his mind, she contends, was more than enough for him to deal with.

Once home, input control was paramount. For years, my mother wouldn't let my sister or me answer the phone. Mom needed to screen his phone calls and make sure only certain ones got through. This required my mother to put all of the information she had into a complicated formula that sorted out the caller, Daddy's state of mind, and the purpose of the call.

She was also very good at telling him only those things he needed to know. My mother quickly learned that the less Daddy knew, the better. She'd lie to him whenever it suited either his interests or hers. She made a point of never giving him bad news if it wasn't something he could fix. Small problems were kept from him because they would send him into a tailspin. But she ran to him with the big stuff because they were his stock in trade. Any problem she had with the rest of the world was always presented to him. It gave him something to focus on, a fight that he could engage in that had nothing to do with her.

Containment, however, was only the beginning. Knowing when and what to say is what allowed my mother to rein him in. Mom never argued with him when he was Disassembled. She understood there was no point trying to talk to him if he was not in the proper state of mind. That meant she had to let go of her own urge to get angry whenever Daddy was in the middle of Disassembling, no matter what it made him do.

Of course, everyone can learn to suck it up when the people they are with are getting scary. There are lots of complacent and tortured people out there who never speak their minds. To me, the remarkable thing about my mother's silence was how deliberate and structured it was. Though she would remain quiet when she knew her words would do her no good, she never let the situation go unattended. My mother could hang on to something forever and never forget to address it. When Pop was prepared to hear it and the right situation presented, she would tell him what she needed him to know. My mother would bring something up a year after it happened, if need be, and do so in a very matter-of-fact tone.

The key to this, my mother says, is *hanging on to the lesson while letting the anger go*. There were never any accusations made, just information imparted. Daddy, a volatile yet practical man, knew how to take these talks.

Of course, reining my father in required more than an occasional comment on wrong conduct. My mother also had to keep him tethered even when he was out of the house. If she did not keep an eye on what he did in the outside world, he could whip himself up into a frenzy that he would eventually bring home. If allowed too much leeway, the mania could overtake him and he would "simply run amok." He could end up just about anywhere and do just about anything. He'd go to the seediest places and get involved with some very unsavory people. So whenever two or three o'clock in the morning rolled around and Daddy had yet to make it home, Mom would get up and track him down.

Once, when Mom got tired of his frequent visits to an illegal gambling operation, she went there to reclaim him. The proprietor came to the door when she knocked and said he wasn't there. So Mom left and came back with a bag full of bricks and lobbed one right through the window. The proprietor sent Pop out, hat in hand, before she let the next one go. She repossessed him from houses of ill repute when the women involved decided he was too much trouble and called my mother at home. She rescued him from men who intended to rob him, and from a few who already had.

I learned of these things gradually over the years after time had taken the sting away from Mom's recollection of them and brought me enough maturity to understand just what they meant. Unfortunately, I cannot do justice to them here. You really need to hear them from her. Much of the beauty is in the telling, in the tone of her voice and the editorial comments. Mom can put you on the floor doubled over with laughter looking back at things that once caused her unfathomable stress, but which have since been emotionally reordered to make them of value now.

In order to fully appreciate my mother's abilities, you not only have to understand what happened, but what didn't happen as well. There are women my father would have abused—physically, and rather badly. I later learned that his first wife didn't fare very well in that department. But Mom knew how to be strong in a way that made him respect the line she drew. Daddy may have been a little nuts, but he certainly wasn't stupid. The prospect of my mother leaving him was not something he could face.

My mother used that to her advantage. She would remind him

of the line she'd drawn. When he was calm enough to hear it as a fact—instead of a threat—she'd tell my father exactly where that line was: "I'm not taking any licks." Though Mom conceded that if she ran and he couldn't catch her that counted in his favor, she made it very clear that the minute one punch connected, she would be out the door. And though she would remind him of her position on occasion, she took care that it didn't hang it over his head. "If you feed anyone's fear too much," Mom explained, "it eventually works against you."

Another thing that didn't happen had to do with my sister and me. This one she did not have to explain to me. I figured it out on my own. Looking back with the vision I have developed through my own motherhood and time, I realize how easy it would have been for Kathy and me to fall through the cracks. Even when he was at his worse, and there was a house full intoxicated guests, Mom had us on her radar screen. "I could not keep them out of the house," my mother said, "but I always knew where they were when they were in it, and I knew where you were, too."

In my mother's mind, we were the point of the whole thing, and she never lost sight of that. Her top priority, my father's antics notwithstanding, was preparing my sister and me for a life outside the asylum. She saw to our total education. There wasn't a sign-up sheet in Columbus that didn't have my or Kathy's name on it. Flute lessons, violin lessons, jazz dance, piano, ballet, gymnastics— you name it, and we were in it. In fact, I remember quite distinctly the day we arrived late to the recreation center and the only class that still had an opening for that summer was baton twirling. I'll give you just one guess what I now know how to do.

Yet another thing my mother didn't do *did* have to be explained to me later, when I was in college. She told me that she'd made it her business to manage the way my sister and I felt about our father. While I had learned in high school that she'd shielded us from the worst of him, I did not understand, until I was told, that she had orchestrated how we perceived what we did see.

"I was not going to let you hate him," she said. "It would have hurt you more than it hurt him." My mother drew my attention to the following things I had not realized when I was young. She never said anything bad about him in front of us. She always explained why he did the things he did. She attributed the ease of our lives to his hard work. And she let him do what he did best for us in a very noticeable way. When the rest of the world had something for us that we didn't like, we were trained to holler "Daddy," sit back, and watch him make it right.

The most important thing that didn't happen, though, was Mom failing. Toni Toler never fell down. She could have taken any one of a million emotional roads to immediate satisfaction, and in doing so lost us along the way. Drinking, drugging, and running off were all viable options. Endless shopping was also available to her, as was any of a dozen other diversions.

But she did not do any of those things. There was no falling into a state of depression, no numbing of her ability to feel. She did not lose her sense of humor nor her ability to care. She did not let Daddy wear her down and she did not become his victim. She did not become angry and she never, ever, took things out on us.

I believe that the reason she was able to avoid all of these pitfalls is that she was able to distinguish between what he did to her and who she was. Her self-esteem, though occasionally bruised, never took a serious blow. My mother kept her eye on the point of the whole thing, no matter how difficult Daddy made it. My mother had places she would not go and things she would not take. And no matter what he did to her, these lines—they never changed.

Of course, this is not to say that things were easy for her. She was exhausted all of the time. Rarely was she happy. Once, she started crying and couldn't stop. It went on for days, she said, a problem of such intensity that my father made her see a psychiatrist friend of his. She kept telling herself throughout the entire episode that there was nothing to cry about. With her Second Set of Eyes, she watched herself with no small amount of amazement as she was being swept away by this emotional flood.

This episode, I believe, was an excellent example of what Mom does best. "Always be aware," my mother always says. "Always have a piece of yourself carved out somewhere that can see exactly what you're doing. That way, even if you're not prepared to stop, you know exactly what's going on. Lying to yourself is the worse thing you can ever do."

Mom went to see my father's psychiatrist friend, but she did not enjoy her visit. Once she realized it was she—and not her husband—that the doctor sought to have hospitalized, my mother suggested that he was talking to the wrong party, got up, and went home.

My mother's emotional deluge was notable because it was so out of character. Always aware of her family's needs, she tended to schedule her sadness. To this day, I cannot abide the sound of Mahalia Jackson's voice. It torments me so because Mahalia was the one who ushered my mother into her occasional surrenders. Sitting on the far right corner of the family room couch, Mom always fell in the same place. There she'd stay, head in hand, with an expression that screamed defeat while Mahalia sang on our high-fi. Standing stock still in the family room door, I'd watch her, but I never interrupted. And though I would like to say that I maintained my silence out of respect for her need, I'm quite sure that wasn't it. Each time I saw it I was terrified that this, indeed, was it. Knowing that if she fell I would go under soon after, I held my breath, wondering, in the selfish way that children do, whether Mom would be all right. But, of course, Mom always got up eventually. Adjusting her emotional response was what Toni Toler did best.

Mom had limits, though. Innate stoicism notwithstanding, she knew when to give ground. Some days you just couldn't do anything with Daddy. Once fully enveloped by his mania, no amount of externally imposed stability could make him stop.

"Wow Pow!" he used to say sometimes. He'd scream those words for no discernable reason. "Wow Pow!" the mania would announce itself, and everyone knew to step back.

Mom would put him out of the house when necessary, and into the hospital when that wasn't enough. I remember once she was frying chicken, paying deliberate uninterrupted attention to cooking this meal while sternly, but quietly, telling a stream of my father's friends who'd come to plead his case, "No, he cannot come back in here. I can't put up with him now."

And, yes, she may even have pulled a gun on him a time or two, but she never even winged him. It was just a show of force to make sure he knew exactly how close he was standing to the line.

Once, my mother got a doctor friend of his to prescribe him some very strong tranquilizers. Unable to get him to take them, she put them in his food. Though typically they would have put a man his size to sleep, all they did to him was render him unable to move. He could still talk, though, and he told Mom, "When I can get up from here, I'm going to kill you." She never did that again.

Guns and tranquilizers notwithstanding, none of that ever went too far. My mother's basic nature would not allow her to get carried away. Focused on the task at hand, she never allowed her emotions to take her past the place she needed to go. All shows of force were calculated to serve a purpose. They were for containment, not for revenge or cathartic release.

There were occasional setbacks, but things continued to get better. The number of drunken parties he hosted began to decline. While he still came home drunk, he started coming home drunk and alone. Eruptions became less spectacular and he started taking orders here and there. I think the sheer force of her unwavering stability helped steady his unquiet mind.

By the time we went to college, Mom had things pretty much in hand. They moved when we left, bought a new house with cash, and put everything in my mother's name. It was about this time that Daddy started preparing for his eventual demise and ensuring my mother's financial security once he was no longer around. He still misbehaved, to be sure, but she always saw him coming. She knew him so well that there wasn't much he could do that she couldn't handle.

I remember once, when I was visiting from college, he said wanted to go somewhere and Mom simply said, "No."

"Everybody's going to be there, Toni," he said, with some heat in his voice.

Her response: "Everybody may, indeed, be there, but this time, everybody does *not* include you."

He walked out of the room in a bit of a huff, then Mom turned and looked at me. "Now fifteen years ago, I could have never done that. He would have lit up like a Christmas tree."

When Mom thought it was time to for him to stop driving, she never told him so. She just took him down to the Bureau of Motor Vehicles and emphatically shook her head "no" behind his back to all of the personnel who were administering tests. The eye test man wouldn't go along, but the guy who actually gave him the driving test did. Mom said she felt horrible as they drove home and Dad said wistfully, "I just don't understand. I really thought I had it."

THE RULES

The Doctrine of Family

My mother saw to our emotional education with the same sense of purpose as she did the conventional one. The next set of rules is based on what my mother did at home. They address the emotions so often implicated when family gets involved.

RULE NUMBER 11: Keep Your Eye on the Point of the Whole Thing

Every once in a while you have to step away from what you're doing and make sure you are still heading in the direction you originally intended to go. Dealing with everyday problems and immediate feelings can obscure your ultimate goal. If you don't keep your eye on the point of the whole thing, sometimes you wander off the path.

Case in Point: I had a lady in my courtroom once charged with child neglect. She had left her three preschool-aged children alone in the car while she went into Sally's Beauty Supply to get hair ribbons for the girls. She stayed in there a very long time and the kids got scared, so they started screaming and someone called the police.

In court, she kept telling me how important her children were to her and how much she wanted them to look good. My question to her was: What good is your child's appearance if some stranger walks off with her? This woman had gotten caught in the details and lost sight of the big picture.

RULE NUMBER 12: Draw a Clear Line

There are some compromises that should never be made and some behaviors that should never be tolerated. This rule requires us to define these things clearly and to stand by those decisions we make. Being cool and calm is one thing; being taken advantage of is quite another.

The thing you have to remember is that all lines drawn must be specific. Concrete things are much easier to understand and thus much easier to defend. "I will not be mistreated," is a hope, not a line, because it's far too vague. "The first time a man hits me I'm out the door," however, draws a clear line.

And while which lines to draw is a decision that must be made by each individual, you are not allowed to draw too many of them, nor are you allowed to draw them too close to yourself. For instance, "I will not tolerate being cut off on the highway" is not a good line to draw, but "I will not lend money I can't afford to lose, no matter how desperate my friend may be," is a good one.

Case in Point: I fell down in 1996. You'll read more about that further on. But suffice it to say I had a bad year for a multitude of reasons. I'd given birth to my second son by then, and I was still a sitting judge. I was doing a lot of community work and I was the president of a club called the Cleveland Chapter of Links.

Then something happened. I'm not sure what, but things took a sharp left turn for me. I became morose and angry. There was a lot of crying involved. Sleep had become a distant memory and I was worrying even more than usual.

Apparently a few phone calls were made, and the next thing I knew Mom drove up to Cleveland from Columbus. She watched me for a few days, helped me with the boys, cooked and cleaned like a slave. Next thing I knew, off to the doctors I went, and I came home with a bottle of "slow happy." Zoloft is its commercial name, but I call it "slow happy" because it doesn't work right away.

Mom had to go home before I felt better, but before she hit the road she talked to me about keeping my eye on the prize. "Half the battle," Mom said, "is remembering what it is you are really trying to do.

"The whole point of this thing is to take care of your kids. If the roof came caving in on you, you'd lay down on top of those boys to protect them from the debris. You can do that now," she said, "even when the fallout is from you."

She told me to identify absolutes and to draw deliberate lines. "Tell yourself out loud what you are unwilling to do. Make it an absolute rule." There was to be no yelling while in the room with your kids. No arguing with my husband, either. I was to call my mother whenever an unusual thought popped into my head. I was to remind myself of what I was trying to do before I gave in to how I felt.

Now was the time to keep my eyes peeled because a whole pack of dogs was on its way to my house. In the land of emotions, awareness is half the battle. Hawk-like vigilance becomes necessary when things are not going well.

Five

Mother's Best Save

I think somehow,
That up till now,
I've been wasting the time I've been spending.

I'm growing old,
And so I'm told,
The best years of life are now ending.

But as of yet,
I'd rather forget,
The things that I've been through sober.

So I've been thinking,
If I start drinking,
Maybe the worst is over.

—Me at 13

Unlike the silence Mom chooses when it comes to her past, she is quite open and vocal about mine. She's willing to entertain just about anyone with tales of my odd behavior, sharing each with a sense of wide-eyed wonder that would make you think she was telling it for the first time. And if you let her, she will conclude her remarks by repeating her favorite familial theory: that on her second go-round she bore fruit that fell just a bit too close to her husband's emotional tree.

"Lynn screamed all of the time when she was a baby," she'll say. Quickly followed by the comment, "But she refused to talk until she was well over three."

"She ran around in circles all of the time, and when I asked her to stop she'd say 'I can't.' In fact," she'll continue, "Lynn ran around and *into* things so often that one grammar school teacher called me in to 'discuss' her inordinate number of black eyes. The school thought I was beating her. Can you imagine that?"

The stories, however, do not end there.

"You know how some babies won't let strangers pick them up?" my mother will say, "Well, Lynn wouldn't let them look at her at all. If a stranger peeked in her stroller or tried to talk to her while she was in my arms, all hell would break loose and she wouldn't stop screaming until they went away."

And then there are the stories she tells about me destroying things. "She'd pick up a bat and whale away at shrubbery until she could hardly stand. She'd take light bulbs out of lamps and smash them against walls."

There were also reports of me wetting myself at interesting times and at an embarrassingly advanced age. My bad memory notwithstanding, even I remember a few of these. Once, when I was ten and standing in the middle of a store, I found myself too afraid to ask my own 15-year-old cousin, Diane, to take me to the bathroom. Paralyzed by the fear of simply making a request, I left the issue unattended for too long. Nature caught up with me before my courage did and that, in the end, was that.

It also happened once when I was at a piano lesson. I peed right on the bench. My age, and my refusal to acknowledge the act, made the sudden presence of liquid difficult for my teacher to understand.

My personal recollection of this particular problem ends there. But Mom says, "Are you kidding?" When I asked her if she remembers more, she simply shook her head.

"Weren't you guys worried about me?" I inquired as I continued to gather information.

"You know, once your Aunt Millie did ask me what was wrong

with you but I didn't understand what she meant," a pause, and then, "and at one point I *did* have to stop your father from calling you a moron because you wouldn't talk."

"But you weren't worried, though?" I press.

"Baby," she said, "I was so used to you, and so overwhelmed by your father, that getting through the day was all I could deal with at the time."

That is, my mother says, until 1966, when the odd angle of ordinary that defined her little girl became too obtuse for her to ignore. One day, my third-grade teacher told everyone to take out their pencils, and I could not find mine. Unable to control the hysteria that followed, Mrs. Dudash sent me home. That was the year I took up residence in the closet and refused to come back out.

I had lost the ability to distinguish between real and ridiculous concerns. It is an embarrassing condition that, on occasion, overcomes me still. When suffering from it I tend to consider all potentially negative outcomes without regard to the likelihood of their occurring. Now I know what to do, but back then I didn't have a clue. So my fears would just cascade on me. Daddy would break out a window and I'd wake up convinced that I was going to die in an automobile accident that day. Yes, these things were completely unrelated, but to me, somehow, they made sense. The practice of excessive worry does not account for probability and does not recognize cause and effect.

In those days, my world was an arbitrary and incendiary place that picked people out at random and burned them alive.

And that's how I ended up in the closet, which, it seems, was just too much for Mom to ignore. The next thing I knew we were off to see Dr. Sherard, some sort of pediatric specialist. Though I remember going, I don't remember much about what happened once we arrived. We sat in chairs in front of his desk and he had on a white coat. I was scared of him and mad at Mom. I had no intention of saying a word. I don't remember if I ever talked to him. Nor do I recall anything he may have said, except one terse, endearing comment he made to Mom. "Leave her alone, Toni," was the remark. "She can kick my desk all she wants."

After he spoke briefly to me, I was dismissed and the two of them had a conversation. Years later, Mom told me what they had said. She had asked him what he thought my problem was and he expressed surprise. "What do you mean?" she reported him as saying. "It's all that shit going on in the house." Dr. Sherard was a close family friend who had known my father for thirty years.

As inadequate as his diagnosis seemed, it satisfied my mother. She never made me go back, nor did she take me anywhere else for help. Apparently, all she was looking for was a little reassurance, someone to tell her that my behavior was a reaction to madness as opposed to a symptom thereof. *She* needed comfort and support, and you can't you blame her for that. One lunatic per household is, I'm sure, more than quite enough.

Whatever her motivation, I was certainly relieved to learn that I did not have to go back. I had a very low threshold for variables in those days. Getting up and going to school was adventure enough for me. I had no intention of adding anything to that schedule, no matter its stated purpose.

Of course, now that I am in my forties and have the luxury of looking back, I think that a little help may have been in order. You have no idea how many walls I bounced off of before I finally landed where I am. Had someone with expertise tried to regulate me then, things may have been a bit easier. I consider that on occasion when I am having a bad day.

So while I was writing this book, I questioned my mother on this very point. "You had to know something was wrong with me. Why didn't you get me some help?"

"I don't know," she said at first. "What difference does it make now?" Then she looked at me and shook her head as if to say, "Child, why do you waste so much time?"

Undaunted, I inquired again, and Mom rolled her eyes. "Are you okay *now*?" is how she responded, and of course, I had to agree.

"Well then," my mother concluded, "I guess I did my job." Then she took a deep breath and gave me that look, the one that said be quiet and listen. This look, by the way, is the one that precedes all of her greatest nuggets of wisdom. It features a wrinkled forehead and widely opened eyes. "If you are looking for absolutes," she said, "you are living in the wrong world. Everybody makes decisions and judgment calls. There are no easy answers. Certainly, I could have done better. There is no one in life that can say any different. But if everything turned out okay, my question is, 'Why ask?'" Then there was another of her dramatic pauses before she added this, "You know, nobody knew your father and you like I did. Are you sure someone else could have done any better?"

Of course, I don't have an answer to that question. I don't think anybody does. You can't backdate knowledge or second-guess alternate endings. Besides, I like the woman that I am; who knows how much of that is a function of what I went through?

What I do know, though, is that, for years, I was shooting through that tube, desperately searching for some solid ground. I wanted to know that A followed B every time, no matter what, but there was precious little predictability to be had on Weyant Avenue.

This, I believe, is what set the stage for my mother's best performance. Moment by moment, scene by scene, she adjusted who I was. In the beginning, she simply kept me upright and in motion no matter how much I wanted to shut down. She would extract me from my room when I stayed too long. She made me go no matter how much I kicked and screamed. She did not allow the fantasies I spun for myself go too long unaddressed. She'd make me back up and rethink things. She'd make me tell the story aloud. She knew that often, your ears could hear ridiculous far more quickly than could an overheated brain.

Understanding that it was the absence of certainty that kept me all wound up, my mother began manufacturing certainties that didn't really exist. Mom used to lie to me all of the time, blithely creating processes, procedures, and guarantees specifically designed to address any expressed concern. She put my sister and me into private school to further her goal of input control. Columbus School for Girls, they called it, aka CSG: small classes, attentive teachers, and more watchful eyes presented less room for error. CSG was my safety blanket. It swaddled me like an infant. My mother thinks it worked wonders. She still gives them money every year.

As I approached adolescence and it became more pressing to get out of my infinitesimally small comfort zone, she introduced me to the concept of "right now." Teaching me to take life in small, manageable doses, she'd say things like, "Right now is what we're dealing with. Let's just get through this one thing. I can't solve it all, but I can solve this, so let's just work with what we know."

She encouraged me to write things down. She was very supportive of my Sylvia Plath stage, lack of talent notwithstanding. I filled reams of notebook paper with unidentified, looming presences and ominous eventualities. I wrote of things I could not name, let alone hope to control. So I made one up and christened him The Beast—not very creative, but descriptive. My most potent image of him was written when I was 12.

> *He followed me to the end of things*
> *Where there was no place left to hide.*
> *And as I ducked and cowered there*
> *And got upon me knees*
> *To ask him if he'd maybe not.*
> *He just slowly slyly smiled and*
> *Laid his heavy hand upon my head.*
>
> —Me at 12

My mother's efforts in those early years permitted me to function. Those efforts got me back and forth to school, kept me fed, and let me sleep. She wasn't able to keep my world from rocking, but she steadied it enough to allow me to walk around. She allowed no pressure where none was necessary; she focused only on that which had to occur. My education was it. Everything else she allowed to fall out of the strictly structured world she helped developed for me, designed to keep me busy while minimizing incoming stimuli. My mother and I both spent a whole lot time keeping the rest of the world at bay.

It was also around this time my mom started easing me toward the mirror. In my early years, I thought everyone around me was confused. I sincerely believed that no one else fully understood the truly precarious nature of the world. I thought people did things and went places only because they did not know how dangerous those things and places were. I believed my sister was a complete idiot because she was happy all of the time.

Mom started chipping away at that. "Don't you see what's happening here?" she said. "Look at what your friends are doing. They are enjoying themselves, trying new things, and they all make it to tomorrow."

Slowly but surely, I began to see what she was showing me. Everybody was, indeed, getting where they were going. Those around me were all making it to tomorrow, just like me, except they were happy when they got there, while I had a headache.

"It's you and not the rest of the world," Mom would say. "You have to learn to live in the world the way it is." She kept that up, and after a time I began to internalize the lesson. I was supposed to start controlling myself instead of trying to control the world.

Of course, acknowledging that I felt a certain way was one thing—stopping it from controlling my life, however, was quite another. "I know how you feel," Mom would say, "but let's put that over here." Then she would form her hands like she was holding a box and moving it from one place to another. Then she'd lay out everything she knew about whatever it was she was trying to get me to do.

"Now, you know as well as I do," she'd say at the end, "that the worst thing that can happen to you over here," and then she'd point in the opposite direction of where she'd put that imaginary box, "really doesn't have a whole lot to do with what's going on over here." Then she'd make a whirling motion with her hands as is she was encompassing the rest of the world. "We're going to leave this box over here. We know it's there but we're going to ignore it. Let's take care of what's happening here and by the time you finish, this thing," she'd point at the box again, "will have disappeared."

In addition to maneuvering me toward the mirror, Mom also

slowly stopped bridging the gap. Knowing that exposure was my next best move, Mom made me try out for cheerleader. She even tried to make me go to a prom. While I gave in on the cheerleader thing, I held firm on the prom. I enjoyed jumping up and down and doing back handsprings. There was ability involved, and to top it off I was the best one on the team. But the prom thing was a matter of principle. I thought the whole thing was quite silly and, what's more, I found boys offensive. I had no intention of learning to giggle, or getting excited about a dress.

My stance on the prom notwithstanding, mom was forever dragging me places. Kicking and screaming, I'd accompany her and then when it was over she'd say, "Now you don't have to be afraid of this anymore. This is something you can do." Having become infamous with Kay, my one dauntless friend, for figuring out ways to tell Mom, "No, I can't go," my mother figured out how to use Kay to plot against me. She'd toss Kay the keys to her car and shove us both out the door.

As I got older, though—say, about 16—my problems shifted a bit. My hysteria waned, but headaches took its place, and I became morose. "You stayed in your room for an entire year!" Mom loves to tell people that. "You started going to bed at 9:00 because I wouldn't let you go to bed at 8:00."

Still writing my sad and sorry poetry, I developed a better eye for everybody else. I was beginning, albeit tentatively, to appreciate myself. While I knew I was often my own worst enemy, I began to get a glimpse of the benefits my own peculiarity would someday provide.

My peek into life outside the box notwithstanding, there was still the small matter of the headaches. One-sided, intense, and impervious to over-the-counter medication, they became so all-consuming my parents feared I had a tumor. So off we went to the doctor once more, only to rediscover what we had known all along. I was, for the most part, a healthy girl who wasn't feeling clearly.

I got a little testy during this period of my life, a state of discontent due in part, I'm sure, to adolescence. Hormones do what they are designed to do no matter what else is going on. They provide a steady undercurrent that can agitate even the well adjusted. Put them under an already unstable girl, and you create a tidal wave.

I recall my last year of high school as a mad dash. Focused on college as if it was the answer to all my woes, my mother and I began to sprint toward it, trying to outrun an impending collapse. While most people worried about getting into a school, my mother and I dedicated our efforts to making sure I lasted long enough to attend.

At this point the small matter of temper began to emerge. At this stage of my life, my first response to all negative input was to run, hide, avoid, and retreat. I didn't want to get involved. But of course, that doesn't always work. Sometimes you have to turn and fight. And I found that, when forced, I could pull a "Daddy" and take things a bit too far. When I got angry in those days I would completely lose my sense of proportion, just like my father would. If someone crossed that arbitrary line in my head, I believed they deserved whatever I inflicted on them.

My mother's concerns increased exponentially now that my Weyant Avenue behavior was seeping out of the house. Usually, my mother felt she had me contained. While the world at large may have perceived me as a bit frayed about the edges, no one outside my house ever really saw how undone I truly was. Mom would shore me up, every day, and send me off to school. Then I'd fall apart when I got home and the next day, Mom would start all over again.

But in 1976, my underbelly got exposed more than she would have liked. Personally, I didn't give a damn, because by then scared had turned into angry and I was just plain mad. I refused to put my picture in the yearbook, even though all seniors got an entire page. I started quitting things—track, gymnastics—and I got into it with a couple of teachers. Phone calls were made; quiet discussions were had. In fact, one conversation in the teacher's lounge took on such an ugly tone that my friend Marion, who had overheard them talking, called me at home to suggest that I not come to school.

I had volunteered more hours in children's hospital that year than anybody else in the city, but when it came time to get the award, I refused to attend the ceremony. I refused to go on the senior trip, even though I got calls from other classmates' mothers begging me to go. Finally, sent to my school's headmaster for a discussion of my attitude, I was left with the forceful suggestion that I should "learn to have a little more fun."

So I went off to college, and that's exactly what I did.

THE RULES

The Principles of Parenting

My mother's favorite comment on modern-day parenting is that too many people are trying to make their children happy instead of making sure they are prepared for life. And in my mother's mind, being prepared includes learning how to deal with what they feel.

RULE NUMBER 13: Make Sure You Are Seeing What You've Got

The reason I am not sitting in some loony bin rocking back and forth, repeating over and over, "It isn't safe," is because my mother saw it coming and wasn't afraid to call it what it was.

There is something wrong with your children. I don't know what it is, but *you* should. The problem is that our love for them often makes us blind. Our natural tendency is to defend them against all comers, including legitimate criticism.

But you can't help your children overcome their weaknesses if you don't know what they are. So you must consciously fight the urge to make excuses for them. Don't give in to the desire to react negatively to a teacher's criticism before you hear her out. Don't just take your child's side in a dispute without knowing what went wrong. And don't blame the bad crowd or another's influence without considering why your kid went along with something stupid. Remember, the bad kids in that crowd have mothers too, and you have to be willing to face the possibility that one of those mothers might be you.

So, every once in a while, take a moment to look at Junior as if he belonged to the lady next door. Search hard for those things he can't do at all and those that he just doesn't do well.

Case in Point: Take, for instance, my youngest son. His sound, middle-class upbringing notwithstanding, he could, quite conceivably, grow up to be a thug. My beautiful, kind, and caring ten-year-old is in love with all things gangster. He is a child who, in a room full of a hundred children, will find the one and only knucklehead and make him his best friend.

He wants to wear his pants slung low and speak a form of English we do not recognize in this house. He and a couple of his like-minded, hoodlum-in-training friends are the ones most likely to be standing in a corner when the end of the school day comes.

I contend, however, that this is not a friend or school or MTV concern. The problem is simply mine. He is who he is, he likes what he likes, and I have to meet him where he lives. I may have to make him take ballet class or flute lessons. But whatever I have to do to temper his proclivities, I will purposely take those things on.

It won't do me any good to blame a bad crowd or the media, because I cannot change those things in time to help my son. As his mother, however, I have a unique opportunity to mold and steer and adjust. It is my job to make sure he gets where he needs to go despite where he wants to be.

RULE NUMBER 14: The Rule of the Rougher Road

You know how when a baby falls and is not quite sure if he's hurt, he'll look at you to see if he should cry or not, and if you laugh he'll laugh too but if you rush to hug him, he will cry? Well, you can teach an older child to be amused by life's mishaps in much the same way.

To construct a childhood for your kids without want or disappointment is misleading. In order to be on your children's team, sometimes you can't be on their side.

So ask yourself this: have you ever let your children stumble a bit and fall along the way so they know that failing isn't fatal and they can learn to do it well? Or do you try to adjust the world for them, getting up in arms every time your kid does not get something that he wants or suffers some negative consequence?

In the end, you have to prepare your children to live in a world that doesn't love them as you do. If you live cool, your kids will be cool, and there is nothing better than that.

Case in Point: In Nashville, Tennessee, in 2004, parents of children who were not on the honor roll complained that their children suffered undue embarrassment from having the honor roll list posted in the school. The next thing you know, lawyers got involved and suggested, according to an Associated Press report, that all forms of recognition for student achievement may be problematic, including: posting outstanding papers on the bulletin board, academic pep rallies, and—get this—spelling bees. In order to make the underachievers feel better, we can't award those who do well. If this isn't a call for gross mediocrity, I don't know what is.

RULE NUMBER 15: It Isn't So Much What You Say

It's easier for people, including your kids, to process criticism when there is nothing at stake. Regaling them with their weaknesses isn't productive when they've just done something wrong, because a whole lot of unproductive emotions get in between them and what you want them to hear. Being defensive, frightened, or otherwise upset doesn't help anyone's listening skills.

Instead, share this essential negative information with them when everything is going well. Say, for instance, the two of you are watching TV, and you see someone sporting a weakness that you know junior has as well. Casually, and in good humor, say something like, "That's the kind of thing you do. Remember when . . ." Fill in the blank, then laugh, and let it go.

Case in Point: I pointed out of the car window one day and called my youngest son's name. "Do you see those people standing on that corner in front of that raggedy house with their pants hanging around their knees?" I asked, "That's exactly where you're going to be if you don't stop cutting up in school. It may be fun, but it doesn't pay well. Compare the way these people live to what you have at home." Then I pause, just like my mother does, for a little dramatic effect, and then in a very light-hearted tone I said, "I'm not telling you what to do. I'm just letting you know."

RULE NUMBER 16: Introduce Them to The Emotional World

Children need to know how to handle more than just their own emotional stuff. They also need to understand the emotional implications of living in the world. They need to know that other people feel and think in ways that might be very different from their own.

The key to this particular rule is giving them information long before they need it, and in a way that does not resemble "telling them what to do." When you do this, you want to be seen as sharing secrets and not restricting their behavior.

Case in Point: I think I was about thirteen or so. My mother and I were sitting in the car on the corner of College and Livingston avenues. And though I don't remember where we had been or what we had seen that prompted this particular conversation, I do remember what she said.

She was telling me about men, using whatever we'd just seen one man do as a springboard for in-depth commentary. She told me why he did what he did and what it said about how men think—making clear that I shouldn't judge their acts according to what seemed reasonable to me. She explained that there was an entirely different dynamic at work for men on the issue of sex. She referred to an intensity of desire that I might never understand that speaks to the best of men almost as loudly as it does the worst.

And then she added, matter-of-factly, that there is a particular brand of this desire that has been known to prompt men to do things they ought not to with their own children.

The important thing about that conversation is not so much what she said but the way in which she said it. She never said a word about what I wasn't supposed to do. In fact, the entire topic was discussed as if it had nothing to do with me at all. It was almost an academic discussion. Information was imparted in a level, nonjudgmental, and unemotional way.

And I absolutely believe that it had the effect my mother had intended. I came away from that conversation feeling like I had just learned something I wasn't supposed to know. That sometime during "the game" that men and women engaged in, my mother had stolen the other side's playbook and let me peek inside for the first of many looks.

▶ *Six*

Misdirected

I knew it was true. Not only had my mother told me—I had seen it for myself. Living with Daddy may have not helped matters, but I knew it wasn't just him. After all, Kathy grew up there too and she hadn't lost *her* mind. Though she got upset when things went bad, there was no getting around it—once something blew over, Kathy knew how to stop being afraid. Unlike me. Fear followed me around, dogging my every step. Clearly, my troubles arose not just from *what* kinds of things I saw, but the *way* in which I saw those things.

These facts notwithstanding, when I left for college I still held out hope that maybe it wasn't me. Could it be that getting away from Weyant Avenue was all I needed to do? Was it possible, I wondered, that when I left Columbus, the Beast would stay behind?

That was the dream I carried with me to Harvard Yard, Fourth Floor Thayer, South, and it was there, amidst the ivy, I was forced to let it go. Within weeks of arriving, I discovered that the Beast I battled in Ohio had come to Cambridge, too. Only now I'd internalized the Beast—she'd become part of me, less an outside force than an internal voice. It appeared that no matter what state my body was in, my state of mind stayed the same.

While reports of generalized joy were coming from Dartmouth, where Kathy was having a wonderful time, I was still engaged in a fight for my life with an enemy no one could see but me. Repeating all the well-known phrases voiced to me at home, my new, part-of-Lynn Beast whispered, "What if," and "It isn't safe." She asked me, "Are you sure?" Same Beast, just different subject matter.

"You're stupid," she snickered. "You are in over your head." This one was completely new. I recall staring at the F on my Chaucer Middle English translation exam, wondering whether I had forgotten how to think. "Or, could it be," The Beast proposed, "you never knew how to think at all?"

Then there was the matter of the opposite sex. Having attended an all-girls' school for the preceding seven years, I hadn't paid them much attention. Certainly, I had seen them from a distance, since my best friend, Kay, clearly found them intriguing. But I was a late bloomer and spent most of my high school years wondering what all of the fuss was about. Boys were so pushy and arrogant. All they ever wanted to do was touch things that didn't belong to them. "Why in the world," I used to think, "would anyone want to get involved with that?"

Once I got to college, though, hormones and proximity began to change my point of view. Within weeks I started to understand what Kay had been trying to explain to me all along. But while I was anxious to start dating, I knew precious little about the people with whom I sought to get involved.

The only black men I really knew were of my father's generation— old-school, hard-working, hard-drinking guys who spent their time at my house shooing me out of the room so they could get down "to business." I had had little exposure to the younger kind. Most of the teenaged guys I knew were white private-school boys.

But now I was faced with a whole new breed of being: the cocky, twentysomething black male whose method of courting, as far as I could tell, did not include requests of any kind. Forceful and unflappable, they remained completely unfazed by my claims of lack of interest. "You should be with me," they'd say. I had no idea what I was supposed to do with that.

New to dating, and relatively new to parts of my own culture, and experiencing grades that resided much farther down the alphabet than to which I was accustomed, I struggled to find my comfort zone. I was away from home. My old problems had yet to resolve and new ones were showing up every day. I was set to spin out of control.

So what did I do? Did I rise to the occasion? Battle back the Beast and overcome Harvard by sheer force of will? Did I keep coming, as my mother had, and accomplish all my goals?

Unfortunately, no.

What I did instead was hide out in my dorm room and break just about every rule my mother ever had. Hanging on to my headmaster's words, I focused on having fun. I found a fearless new friend whose name was Janice. Nothing bothered her. So I learned to cope with new and scary by letting her go first.

I did little beyond sleep, eat, and attend the occasional party. I pursued joy like it was a job. Not recklessly, mind you, the Beast would not allow that, but with a sense of entitlement. Anything that did not require too much effort, wouldn't kill me, or wouldn't get me arrested was the order of the day. I have never known this before, I reasoned; I am due a little fun. So with no small measure of righteous indignation, I dilly-dallied and tip-toed my way out of college, picking up very little of what I had been sent there to learn.

This was a very unfortunate choice, a stupid and costly mistake. I was given an opportunity very few get and I chose not to take it. If I'd had the maturity I have today, I would have sucked up everything within reach. But I did not have the presence of mind to truly understand just what I was throwing away.

That is not to say that I didn't learn anything at all at Harvard. I did learn quite a lot, in fact. Regrettably, not much of it came from the institution to which my father was paying tuition. Instead, my college education primarily consisted of information I could have gotten completely free of charge. I learned all of my best lessons over the phone discussing the problem of the day with Mom.

Looking back it all makes sense, though I did not have a clear vision of it at the time. In Mommy 101 (those things I learned while at home), my mother had been teaching me how to live with myself. She was teaching me how to stand upright when I would have preferred to fall down. But now, in the more advanced Mommy 201, I began to learn about others: people and society, men and women, black and white—these were the lessons Mom gave me over the phone.

Early on in this process, my mother established her qualifications for advanced instruction by infallibly predicting the behavior of many people she didn't know. It was as if my mother had spent some time living in everyone else's head. Her wisdom, I discovered, was not confined to Weyant Avenue, as I had once assumed.

My phone calls home were plentiful and filled with all kinds of ridiculous things. I didn't know what to do with the boys who demanded instead of asked. Nor did I have a clue what to say to the ones I liked. As a result, the ones I didn't want kept hovering around, and those I did want just walked away.

"How does that happen?" I wanted to know. "Why can't they hear what I actually say?"

Then there were a few of the other girls—not many, but enough—who seemed to dislike me for reasons I could not comprehend. The nicer I got, in fact, the worse they treated me. So Mom taught me about jealousy and the misinterpretation of shy. "They think you are a stuck-up bitch," Mom said, "They don't know that you're just scared and odd." Thus she began on the value of understanding how what you do looks to others. She then began showing me how to step away from myself to better watch what's going on.

"I can take myself out of any situation I'm in," Mom says. "I can turn down my own emotional static well enough to hear everyone else's." It is this process by which you train yourself to first identify and then set aside your own feelings, so that you can concentrate not just on what the other guy is saying, but what he is feeling as well. These were some very important lessons in creating what became my Second Set of Eyes.

This is not to say that I was the perfect student. Mom warned me about a couple of things that I went and did anyway. One had to do with an older guy who failed to mention his longtime girlfriend until I was already in over my head. It ended just as she said it would. When he was finished, he walked away.

Mom never said I told you so. Instead, she made sure I learned the best lessons I could from that mistake. What she wanted me to take away from the experience had very little to do with men. Though she may have made a vague reference to the tricks of the trade, the main point that she sought to make dealt with me alone. "He was at fault for leading you on until the day he told you about her. But the moment you knew, everything changed—*you* became the one responsible."

Here is the greatest lesson Mom taught me during this time. It all started one day when I was overcome by a wave of regret regarding my $200,000 "vacation." I told Mom all about the things I didn't learn while I was at school. I owned up to how lazy I had been and how I had truly spent my time. While confessing, though, I suggested in my own defense, that I had needed "time to decompress." After all, my reasoning went, I had had a difficult childhood. Anyone would need some time to blow off steam after the things that I had gone through.

Mom rolled her eyes.

"You can lie to me all you want," she replied, "but whatever you do, don't lie to yourself." Mom said that a lot. It was how she avoided passing judgment on me, by making me do it myself. We had a long conversation about my college days and what they said about me. Through Mom's lens, I saw that I'd learned how lazy and complacent I could be. College had exposed my desire to hide from unpleasantness. My behavior suggested a need for greater passion in the absence of parental control. I needed to really want something beyond just getting away from home. I was not, it seems, self-motivated. I needed a little push.

We went through it, my mother and I, and when we were done the final lesson was this. "Now that you've done it and know what it's about, you don't get to do that anymore." Error without regret is okay, *if* the lesson is fully learned.

"What now?" of course, was the next question. My options in answering it, however, were few. Graduate school was a foregone conclusion in my house. At no point did my parents ever allow me to consider college the end of the line. The question was simply *which* graduate school to attend, not whether or not I would. I could do anything I wanted as long as I ended up a doctor or a lawyer. Much to my parents' dismay, I chose what they considered to be the lesser of the two. My sister, who to date had been the least likely to do what she was told, was the one to get it right and go to medical school.

The easier course notwithstanding, there was still the issue of getting accepted. Having misbehaved for the past four years, my grades were nothing to write home about. That being said, considering the level of my participation, I didn't do that bad. I bought the books, crammed for the exams, and had always been a quick study. More importantly, however, I was a whiz at taking standardized tests. I did very well on my LSATs. So I got into the University of Pennsylvania Law School—still Ivy League, but as my father once pointed out, not quite as Ivy as he would have liked.

Once there, however, I realized that I was a bit of a slow learner with respect to several things taught in Mommy 201. In law school, I fell right back into all of my the bad habits I had in undergrad. I didn't like law school. Most law students don't. It is not a fun place to be. Be that as it may, my reaction to its unpleasantness was all wrong. I chose, yet again, to do some very stupid things.

The first mistake I made was trying to quit, but that didn't work out at all. When informed of my desire to leave, Daddy responded with quiet calm. He said I could do anything I wanted, but that as soon as I stopped going to law school, he would stop sending me money. Unstable, yet not a silly girl, I decided to stay the course. I knew I wasn't ready to support myself in the style to which I had become accustomed.

Realizing that quitting was not an option, I landed on my second brilliant plan. Do nothing, just like you did in college, but this time worry more. Like always, I found myself one friend who kept me from spiraling completely out of control. Her name was Trisha; she was very smart and she tolerated my oddness. She hated law school just as much as I did, but she had enough sense to attend more classes.

I also found me a man who was willing to put up with me most of the time. His name was Jim. He was a good guy; he always tried to make me work. The best I could manage, though, was buying the textbooks and making occasional appearances in class. This was enough to keep me in school without too much exertion.

It was not, however, enough to keep the Beast from thinking up something new.

Though I was having a little trouble associating my failure to attend class with an ultimately unpleasant outcome, my Beast understood it all too well. She had a very firm grasp on the relationship between what I wasn't doing everyday and what I eventually wouldn't know. She always saw every potential negative tomorrow in Technicolor detail. But though she saw the situation clearly, the Beast's response was predictably bad. The Beast recommended worry instead of action. She told me to stay in my apartment and think about everything that was going wrong. The Beast, I learned, does not believe in *doing* anything, because action saps her strength.

The Beast had a field day in Philly. She and I sat around my apartment and conjured up all kinds of interesting concerns. Eventually, I became so consumed by the *process* of worry that I had a hard time discerning real problems from the ones I'd just made up. It was like being nine years old all over again even though I managed to stay out of the closet this time. The world was precarious, mercurial, and cunning. I saw nothing but imminent demise.

On several occasions I tumbled into some fantasy disaster and had a hard time finding my way out. Once I became convinced that I was going to burn down the apartment building in which I lived. I then decided that since my father co-signed the lease, he would be held responsible for the damage. This, in turn, would cause him to lose everything he'd worked so hard to get. I distinctly recall one 3 A.M. lecture by my boyfriend, Jim, in which he informed me that under no circumstances was he going to get out of the bed again and take me home to see if I turned off the gas. I sat up all night in his living room until it was light outside and then I caught the bus home.

Then there were the illnesses. I took every itch and twitch, sneeze and ache as a sign of imminent death. Of course, this was a personal thing I learned the hard way not to share.

Jim almost passed out laughing the day I told him I had lockjaw. He knew that I was serious but he just couldn't help himself. I kept subsequent medical scares to myself. I never mentioned my suspected brain tumors, angina, and (believe it or not) amyotrophic lateral sclerosis (Lou Gehrig's disease). You'd be amazed by the body of medical knowledge one can gather, and subsequently misinterpret, in a very short period of time.

When the worry became too much for me to handle, I always called home. Breathless and animated, I'd rant about the latest disaster, real or perceived. Mom would listen intently as I explained how some minor difficulty was about to destroy my entire world. She never challenged the logic of anything I said. She'd skip right over all of that and get right to the core. "Now you're all off," she'd tell me, "None of that makes any sense. You're worried and you're on a roll, and we just can't entertain it."

Reminding me that my real fight was with an enemy within, and not whatever it was that had me so riled up, she'd conclude our conversations with instructions to do one small specific thing. I was then told to call her the next day, once that thing was done. This way I had a deadline for doing it, and she could talk me up some more and send me out to do something else.

I believe that's the best thing I learned while I was in law school. There, I learned to piece a life together by limiting my range of thought. All fears not actively engaged with productive action were to be dismissed. I actually envisioned a beast tied to a chair and placed in another room. "Right now," was the phrase I kept repeating. Sometimes I said it out loud. Even if it wasn't true, I told myself that if I took care of this "right now," then tomorrow would take care of itself. I learned that focus fostered calm and kept the Beast at bay.

THE RULES

The Continuing Education Requirements

You will have to continue to learn about yourself all of your life. You never arrive. The whole thing is a process, and the process doesn't end until you die.

RULE NUMBER 17: Beware the Comfort of Deciding It's Not Your Fault: The Rule Against Teching

Technically, you can get away with a lot of stuff. There are usually several factors that contribute to any problem. As a result, you can almost always find someone or something, other than yourself, to blame for the ones you have—"technically." This can lead to "Teching." Teching occurs when you search through a mess that *you* made for one small thing that somebody else did wrong.

The Rule Against Teching says you don't get to do that. Ever. In fact, it requires you to go out of your way to identify any part you played in the problems that you have, even when those of others are more inviting, profitable, or prominent. In fact, even if your problems are 99 percent someone else's fault, make sure you look hard for and accept the 1 percent that's your own. That 1 percent may be what keeps your problems from becoming a tragedy. It may be that last step not taken that would have put you over the edge.

If you blame others, you might get some sympathy.

If you accept responsibility, you gain control.

Case In Point: Teching is what got Lisa and Grandma Anne into all that trouble, and what brought them before my bench. Lisa was 24 or so, had three small children, was not employed, and was living in Grandma's house. One night, Grandma came down stairs and caught Lisa having sex on the couch. With what I am sure were visions of yet another mouth to feed dancing in her head, Grandma approached the coupling pair and objected to the proceedings.

Lisa responded by picking up a knife and chasing Grandma all over the house.

Once in court, Lisa pled guilty to assault, admitting (off-handedly) that attempting to slice up Granny was not the thing to do. Unfortunately, however, her brandishing a knife was very low on her list of concerns. Instead, she was much more animated about the way the police handled the situation when they arrived.

"Yes, my grandmother told the police I had a knife when she called," she said, "And yes, I threw a high chair at the cops when they came in the door. And, yes, I refused to be handcuffed, but I still don't think they had a right to wrestle me to the ground." She then went off on a tirade in which she posed her considered opinion that the police should never get physical with women.

Thinking that Lisa was due for a wake-up call, I called Grandma Anne to the bench for a little reinforcement, expecting an emotional account of the outrage that had occurred in her home. Had I been thinking clearly, however, I would have known better. What happened instead was very logical, disheartening though it may have been. Grandma Anne came up to the bench, said not a word about her granddaughter, and started in on the police as well.

Grandma Anne was a victim of Teching. Having searched the perimeter of her problems for someone else to blame, she worked hard to avoid an opportunity to fix what was really wrong.

RULE NUMBER 18: Do Not Believe the Lies You Tell Other People

People tend to make a lot of excuses for what they do. No one likes to feel stupid, nor is it any fun to admit that you are wrong. Though excuses make you feel better, that sense of relief comes at the cost of control. And if you lose too much of that, you go into "victim mode."

If you need to move the truth around a little in order to keep from looking like a fool in front of others, well, go right ahead. Exposing your weaknesses is a very high-order behavior and most people just can't do it. If, however, you do choose to massage the facts, you must still make a clear, concerted, and conscientious effort to remember and believe the truth. Your brain has an amazing capacity for believing the lies it tells. It likes consistency and gets habituated quickly, so it can reorder what you know in an effort to make it consistent with what you want to believe.

A lie can actually start feeling like the truth if you tell it often enough. And if you don't pay attention, the day may come when you can no longer tell the difference between the two.

Case in Point: I had a guy I'll call Joe in my courtroom one day. Arrogant, angry, and unapologetically macho, he refused to answer any of my questions. Leaning back on one leg and shrugging his shoulders, he came off as very unconcerned.

Seeing that I was getting nowhere with my usual tactics, I leaned over the bench and whispered loudly into the court microphone, "You know, your Joe Cool routine is a good one, but it's a little out of place. You're a 37-year-old man living at home with your mother and when you asked her to use the car, you shoved her around because she said no.

"Under the circumstances," I continued, "I'm quite confident that, no matter what you do, you can't pull the cool thing off."

Joe actually hung his head and laughed. He had been playing the role so long he had started believing it himself.

Seven

The Corrected Course

In October, 1984, the First National Bank of "Daddy, Can I Have" officially closed its doors. I was working at a large law firm in Cleveland when Daddy called to say he was done. Pointing out that I had a law degree, a job, and no debt at all, he wanted to make it clear that no more money would be coming my way from Columbus.

At the time, I thought it was an odd thing to do. I had already assumed this was the case. But he made the call, I heard him out, and I took it as it was intended—only to learn, years later, that Daddy had not meant what he said at all.

One day, Mom and I were drinking wine when the subject of that phone call came up. "We didn't really mean that, you know," she said. "We just wanted to make sure you conducted your business like we weren't there." They were, as my mother calls it, "getting my mind right." After all, they had been caring for me all of my life. They wanted to make sure that I was making a conscious emotional adjustment to being on my own.

Money, however, was the least of my concerns. I was, and always have been, cheap. With me, money made was money kept, so it was never much of an issue. Unfortunately, however, just about everything else was. It seems the Beast was none too pleased with my new position in the big bad world.

I found the sheer quantity of effort involved in keeping a job to be a new and interesting thing. When I got stressed out at school, I simply stayed in my room. But now I had to keep showing up in order to get paid. That's a hard thing to do when you're in the habit of putting a microscope to the world, forever eyeballing the details, and hoping to identify any harm (no matter how small) before it falls your way. It's tiring, especially when you are required to hide it from everyone you know.

The loneliness, too, was unprecedented. You don't need many social skills to find people to hang out with in school. Now, though, I was single in what I learned was a very married city. Here, effort was necessary in order to have a social life. But I hated going out. The Beast did not want me to meet new people. "They could hurt you," she would warn. So I went to work and then came right back home, a habit that kept me dateless and friendless for more than two years. This, in turn, gave the bitch in my brain something new to play with. Sidling up to me one day, she asked, "Is this all there is?"

Until then, I had spent my entire life just trying to get through things. I took life in three- to four-year chunks, which made its bitter taste easier to swallow. No matter how upsetting my current problems were, I took solace in the fact that I knew when they would end. Four years and high school would be over; four more years, then, to finish college. And law school, thank God, lasted only three. In short, I had been surviving on the knowledge that "this too shall pass," but now that I was working there was no place else to go. "This is *it*," I thought, and promptly sank into a sadness I had not seen since I was fourteen. What was I to do with all of this fear, all of this unhappiness, now that I had no place else to go?

When informed of my new melancholy, Mom expressed frustration. Even a woman as emotionally well managed as she has limits to her patience. I imagine I heard one of her favorite sayings a lot around this time: "The world is not going to adjust to you, you have to adjust to the world." The theme of her commentary around this time was simple: *Get your act together.* She made it clear that if I was unhappy, I had to address what it was about *me* that made the world seem such an unfriendly place. Then we embarked together on yet another new emotional journey designed to acclimate me to the world.

The first and most important lesson she taught me was how to do things in the right order. I learned that this meant I would have to do certain things long before I *wanted* to do them. I could not, she explained, wait until I wanted to go out before I actually did. Instead, I had to make myself go out, and get used to it; the wanting would come later. She told me to watch other people who had good social lives, and imitate what they did. "Just pick one thing they do," she told me "and then you do it, too. Once you have that one down and start seeing some results, just pick out another one and do it all over again."

My mother then began to emphasize the need for picking a passion. I was, she informed me, too goal-oriented. I always needed to feel like I was getting somewhere in order to have fun. So it was my job to find a passion to pursue, so that I would have something to get excited about. The world, she told me in no uncertain terms, had no obligation to entertain me.

So I struggled. But notably, I never fell down. There were no bizarre imagined illnesses or breathless phone calls at all hours of the night. There was a sense of steadiness that lay beneath the angst this time. This I claimed as a victory, hard won through years of practice. I kept moving and maintained my composure no matter how I felt. I learned to piece a life together out of my few social skills.

I was inching toward the outside, one small step at a time, when two things happened to me—much as they had happened to my mother years before.

When I was hired, I was the only black female attorney in my 200-lawyer firm. Two years later they hired another. Sonali and I have been friends ever since. We were both rarities in every world we entered. She is the friend I would have ordered if you could do those kinds of things. Both born black to upper-middle-class circumstances in homes with no small measure of drama, she and I were alike in more ways than I could count, with one very meaningful exception: Sonali was simply fearless. Very little bothered her. She knew how to take on life, and she did so with aplomb no matter what the problem was. So like I had with Janice, I let her go first, and then I followed right along.

Then, one day in 1987, I was asked to attend a basketball game. My firm was entertaining a group of judges and two of them were black women, so they decided to trot me out. One of these judges was Stephanie Tubbs Jones. When I was introduced to her, she did not say hello or ask me how I was doing. The first thing out of her mouth was, "Do you have somebody?" and the moment I told that woman "no," my entire future was set.

As luck would have it, one of her best friends had just gotten a divorce. She thought meeting me might cheer him up. I married him two years later.

This was significant, and not only for the reasons marriages usually are, but also because of the shift it created in my relationship with my mom. My mother did not want me to marry the guy I picked. In fact, she and I fell out right after I fell in love. We never really argued or anything, but we had a lot of short intense conversations. I realize now that she wasn't really mad at me, but rather with the Beast, which, she believed, was about to author my latest and greatest mistake. She thought that my search for security had caused me to pick a man who had a serious daddy factor going, but not much else to recommend him.

I understood her point completely. His statistics weren't good, and had I been in her shoes I would have objected, too. He was almost but not quite divorced, as the papers had yet to be signed. He had four sons, ages 9 through 17, and very little money. Being the practical woman she was, Mom contended that I had lost my mind.

She was right about some aspects of it. I was looking for the Rock of Gibraltar, and Eric qualified for the job. My husband simply never rattles, no matter how much I shake his cage. He was strong where I was weak. Being with him made me feel safe. He was exactly what I was looking for, all wrapped up in a very pretty package. Six foot one, milk-chocolate brown, with an ass that, to this very day, stands at attention like a marine.

Where my mother and I differed was the wisdom of basing my choice of husband on this need. My mother saw it as a weakness to work around. I saw it as something that needed to be satisfied.

We discussed it endlessly, and when I could not be persuaded, we stopped talking for a while. Silence, we decided, was better than chasing each other around on an issue that might make either or both of us angry.

Eventually I married Eric despite my mother's concerns, and we embarked on a life together that neither one of us had really planned. We had a number of immediate problems, most notably my failure to introduce him to the Beast before he said "I do." Had he known about her, he may never have said it. But now it was too late.

Of course, there are some things you cannot hide from a man you are dating. The edges of my oddness were clearly visible, but I looked good enough back then to get away with that sort of thing. He saw moody. He saw startled. He saw loner, and he saw testy. But he never caught a glimpse of unwound, depressed, or catastrophe-prone. While we were dating, I simply made myself unavailable when things got bad. He'd call and I would refuse to see him, no matter what he wanted.

Once we were married, though, I couldn't hide the Beast any more. She moved right in with us and scared the poor man to death. He had absolutely no idea how trying I could be. Nor did he understand how much alone time I would need. He wasn't prepared for the day some two weeks after we married that I went back to my apartment so I could sleep alone. We hadn't had a fight or anything. I just wanted to be by myself. So I returned to the apartment I had yet to give up. Worse yet, I had the nerve to mistake his stunned silence for understanding and acceptance.

Looking back, I can also recall how bewildered he'd look when I'd take some small concern and turn it into a calamity. Sometimes it's hard to tell when I take a left turn in logic, and rational turns into something else. If nothing else, I am persuasive, and if he didn't watch out I would have him walking down an emotional road to nowhere.

That said, I must point out that I wasn't the only one who brought issues to our marriage. He owned a money problem—a beast of his own that he'd failed to introduce to me. When our two beasts finally met, there was quite a bit of unpleasantness. Not much screaming, but a lot of icy silences and biting comments. I spent a lot more nights alone.

Then, of course, there were the boys, the four young men that walked behind him when we walked down the aisle. They were good kids. Thank God. Absent that, I don't think the marriage would have survived. They seemed to harbor no resentment whatsoever against their dad's new wife, a young woman barely ten years senior to the oldest of them. But there they were, five people in a house with a woman who'd always preferred being alone. I remember calling a girlfriend from my office in hysterics one day, screaming, "I've got nowhere to go!"

And, of course, Eric had emotional issues, too, just like everyone does. There is no such thing as baggage-free in life. He had mammoth trust issues resulting from his first marriage. He always kept an over-sharp eye out for any signs of disloyalty and disrespect, and for a while he saw them everywhere. I could never do or say anything without him filtering it through his "can I trust her?" screen.

Overwhelmed. This was my primary emotion around this time. I was overwhelmed by living with four teenaged boys and a guy who, on occasion, turned into a teenaged man. I was overwhelmed by the fact that, for the first time in my life, money was a problem. I was overwhelmed by the new reality that someone else's problems could have such a big effect on me.

Overwhelmed, however, did not stay alone long—isolated soon joined the party, too. Newly estranged from the one person in life I had always felt most connected to, I felt like I was hanging on a laundry line and flapping in the wind. How could I call my mother *now*, and complain about the consequences of what I fought her so hard to do? She had predicted every pain and problem I now had, but I did not listen to her. It takes a whole lot of woman to slink back to home base after the way I'd dismissed her concerns. Either that or a whole lot of trouble, and in my case, the second one applied. After a while, things got so messy that there was nothing I could do *but* call Mom. I was out of money, out of patience, and neck deep in challenges I never asked for and never expected. Well fed, the Beast had grown too large to handle; she had begun parceling out my sleep at a meager three to four hours at a time.

Breathless and agitated, I relayed to Mom every problem I had, real, imagined, or (as was most often the case) somewhere in between. I was relieved Mom never said "I told you so," even though we both knew she had. Nor did she proclaim "it's not my problem" when I swallowed my pride and asked her to pay our mortgage. What she did, instead, was write the check, and warn me, "Whatever you do, don't tell your father." She then took on every problem I had as if it were her own. Realizing that the "don't marry Eric" ship had sailed, she knew the destination had not changed; she still wanted me to end up happy, so she decided to help me navigate the huge and leaky boat she had begged me not to board.

Easing back into that steady state that had defined our relationship for three decades, my mother and I dealt with my situation with only the point of the whole thing in mind. She taught me a whole new set of rules to help me solve the new set of problems that I had chosen.

Those emotional lessons began, as most do, with a quick trip to the mirror. Until this point in my life, my only real concerns had been traits related to educational and commercial success. Everything I'd done, for the most part, was geared to staying upright and providing for myself. But now I needed to learn emotional lessons designed to help me live with others in close quarters— without my mom on the scene to help manage me.

I needed to learn a number of things, starting with how to assess other people's needs and wants, even when *they* didn't know what they were. I also had a whole *lot* to learn about the way men feel about things. I had to figure out when what my husband did and said to me was really all about something else.

Thankfully, Eric and I made things work, despite all dire predictions to the contrary. The truth is, we went to a marriage counselor once when things got really ugly. He gave us a test to see how amenable we both were to the institution of marriage. If you scored a 10, that meant you were a perfect mate. Scores totaling

5 through 7 were average. Eric scored an inauspicious 4. Me? I got a 1.7. Expert opinion: not a snowball's chance in hell. We've been married 18 years now.

Of course, I'm not claiming that Eric and I are now living Claire and Cliff Huxtable's lives. We are a work in progress—a work that doesn't always work very well. There are still days when the worst in both of us run into one another and start a lot of trouble, but we know enough about ourselves not to let it go too far. More importantly, we don't expect to be happy everyday—just more often than not.

THE RULES

The Doctrine of Family II

RULE NUMBER 19 : Understand the He, Me, and We of It

There are three people in any marriage. You, your spouse, and the thing you become when the two of you get together. When you get married, you *must* change. Things that worked well when you were single will not necessarily work any more. You have to look to see how the best and worst of you brings out the best or worst in the other person. Then you must adjust what it is you do so that things work out the way you want and need them to, for the both of you.

Case in Point: One day, Mom hit me in the head with a pillow and said, "You had better stop apologizing to him." Then she pointed out that one of my better traits had combined with one of my husband's less admirable ones and turned into a mistake.

All my life, Mom had trained me to look at Lynn Toler first whenever anything went wrong. Unfortunately, my husband thought that was a fine idea, and began blaming me for every problem that *he* had. So every time something went wrong, I would admit to any part I played in it, no matter how insignificant or small. My husband would then seize upon that point as the sole focus of his concerns. It got so bad that one day he blamed me for the fact that he'd forgotten his wallet, even though I wasn't with him when he did it. "If you would let me open up the window at night and get some air," he said, "I'd sleep better and wouldn't forget things." Thus identified as the biggest problem in his life, I became the target of all his anger.

So even though taking responsibility is a good thing, in general, I had to change. I had to be much more careful about saying *mea culpa* so he'd stop seeing me as the be-all, end-all bitch who was the source of all his problems.

RULE NUMBER 20: The Rebound Emotion Rule

Rebound Emotions are what hang around a house and make people behave in a manner they never would out in the world. They are what stand in between you and what's happening now in order to show you yesterday. They are emotional background noise that will keep you from hearing what was said, so you can stick instead with what you think.

Rebound Emotions emerge when people get used to feeling a certain way about other people—especially the ones they live with. And after a while, no matter what the other person does, it will be interpreted in a way that fulfills old expectations. Once Rebound Emotions get involved, people stop arguing about specific things, even though they keep on arguing.

A decision has to be made when Rebound Emotions are ricocheting around a house. Someone has to resolve to stop talking about the outrage of the moment and instead begin to address the overall emotional ride. This must be done when no one is angry. You must simply start a conversation about the entire scope of things. And when you do, start with the positive and talk about how you'd like things to be. Then tell everybody that with a little work, you think it can really be that way. Then *you* make the first compromise before you ask for one in return.

Who knows? It may or may not work, but why not give it a try? One kind gesture won't make you weak, and you can always go back to being a jerk tomorrow.

RULE NUMBER 21: The Turn-Signal Requirement

People are a lot less likely to run into you if they know where you're going. You put your turn signal on while driving, and you should use it at home as well.

You get what you ask for. People know what you tell them. They will understand what you explain. Just because somebody loves you doesn't mean he or she can read your mind. Your family cannot do right by you unless they know what that entails.

Never underestimate the value of having a rational conversation, one that occurs right after sex, a satisfying meal, or an unexpected compliment. This should be a conversation that expresses what you want in a nonthreatening, but serious, manner and you should have this conversation *before* you do whatever it is that your partner may not be expecting.

By the way, never assume someone else would have done things differently if they only cared. You'd be amazed at how much stuff that's huge to you can slip right by somebody else. So you have to tell them, and you have to tell them in a manner that does not express your disappointment at the fact that they don't know. You can't get mad because the people you care about are just as human as you.

Case in Point: I have begun a number of marital conversations with the simple phrase, "Honey, I'm just letting you know ..." I have found it to be very helpful.

▸ *Eight*

Karma is a Bitch

My father finished dying on July 10, 1994, a process he claimed to have started sometime in 1988. He had support for this position. All of his doctors agreed. By the late 1980s, both Daddy's heart and his liver were acting up, preparing us all for the day when they would simply shut down. And as if this wasn't bad enough, his great gray masterpiece—his brain, the home of his 144 IQ and his dynamic personality—joined in his body's betrayal. He had a number of small strokes around then that forced him to retire.

After each new heart attack or stroke, Daddy was sent home to await an imminent fate that ultimately took five years to arrive. Year after year, one by one, Daddy made a liar out of each of his doctors. He just kept going and going, in what my mother contends was simply a matter of will.

Daddy, however, did not agree. He said that he *couldn't* die because my mother wouldn't let him. He claimed that she kept doing things that required him to stick around. For instance, once while he was going over his will, Mom said she was going to have a funeral for him whether he liked it or not. He, in turn, slammed his fist on the table.

"That's why I can't die!" he said, "God damn it, Toni—I'm not going to leave you all of this money and let you fuck it up."

Daddy thought nothing of dying. It was all a big joke to him. A confirmed atheist, he believed that when you died, all that mattered was how much money you left behind. He had his demise all planned out so no one would, as he put it, "rip your mother off." He contracted with Ohio State University to retrieve his body. His will specifically provided that there was to be no viewing or funeral. He also contracted with a funeral home (he thought undertakers were all crooks who preyed on grieving families), prepaying for limos to the memorial service my mother insisted on, but insisting that no other money was to be spent.

While Daddy was arranging his final farewell, I was planning a new person all together. In 1991, my husband and I decided we were going to have a baby. Truth be told, I had wanted one since the day that we got married. At 29, the tick-tock of the biological clock starts getting very loud. But Eric kept telling me that we needed time to be alone—or at any rate, as alone as two people can be while co-parenting four children from a previous marriage. There were, he knew from experience, some tough rows to be hoed before we added further complications to our life together.

But I got the go-ahead in late summer of 1991, so I hunkered down, lotioned up, and took on procreation like, as my husband was fond of saying, a full-time job. A good job, he admitted, but a job nevertheless. It is his contention that my single-minded focus on goals can take the fun out of just about anything, and he's right, I have been known to take things a little too far. But since I wanted to have my baby in the beginning of the summer months, I only had a three-month window in which to pull this thing off. Control—my drug of choice—never stops calling my name.

I got pregnant in October and immediately called home. Informing Daddy of his impending grandfatherhood, I told him that I expected him to live long enough to see the baby born.

"Well damn, Lynnie, when are you due?" Daddy asked, as if he had been incredibly inconvenienced.

Despite my father's agitation, I was a very happy woman around this time. Pregnant right on schedule, I had done just what I planned, and I felt very much in control. My mother was ecstatic. It bridged whatever gap remained between us as a function of my marriage. There is nothing quite like a grandchild to bring an uncertain mother-in-law on board.

My joy blossomed for about two weeks. Around the third week of pregnancy, however, I began to realize what it all really meant.

I was going to have to relinquish my drug of choice, cold turkey. I would have to give up control. Once again, I thought I'd lose my mind.

William Livingston Mumford Toler started telling me what to do long before he was born. My body was now his playground. It no longer belonged to me. As it (my body) blew up, I threw up. My nose would bleed for no reason. Trying to hold on to a little boy anxious to exit my person prematurely, I found myself in the hospital quite a lot. I went into labor for the first time at around six months. They pumped me full of magnesium sulphate to stop the contractions, and I thought a truck had hit me. Then they sent me out of the hospital with a needle in my leg and a continuous tributaline pump. I went back several more times before they decided he was old enough to make it on his own. So they took me off the anti-contraction medicine, and for more than a week, nothing happened at all.

Finally, on June 11, 1992, I went into labor. Twenty hours passed; the contractions were intense, but Billy was unmoved. Then his heart rate slowed and I ended up getting a caesarean section because this baby, who threatened for months to come too early, had now decided he wasn't going to come out at all.

Now that my body had been returned to me, I looked forward to feeding my control addiction again. After all, I had been reading baby books throughout my pregnancy. They're experts, I reasoned about the authors (I had yet to fully develop my theory on these people), and if I learned enough of what they knew I should be ready for anything. Besides, Mom was available by phone. What else could any new mother need?

Less than a week later I was ready to throw in the towel. I found that I had given birth to a six-pound, nine-ounce bundle of discontent. Billy was a loud, unhappy baby who wanted to be fed every hour and a half, twenty-four hours a day. Particular about the company he kept, he refused to be held by anyone but me.

"Yep," Mom said, "That's just the way you were. You never slept. Everything upset you and I was the only one who could hold you."

Based on this, my first experience of motherhood, I have been known to contend that karma is, indeed, a bitch. My sister, now a doctor board-certified in neurology, has proffered an alternate explanation. "Shadow traits" is what she called it. It appears that not only am I a chip off the old block, but my oldest son is as well. Whatever illusions I didn't leave in Harvard Yard vanished when Billy Toler was born. He is, I believe, what I would have been had I not lived with Dad, still predisposed to panic and designed, it seems, to worry. Sometimes my heart aches for him as I watch his desperate attempts to control the world. Asking question after question, my son can drive you crazy with "What if" and "Is this safe," picking apart any situation so he will leave nothing unknown or to chance. I understand just how he feels and it hurts me to know just how hard everyday things are for him.

But I digress. We were talking about his early days. Things were tough in Cleveland then and they weren't much better in Columbus. Having seen his namesake born, Daddy went back to the business of dying. In fact, the first time he saw him, Billy was three weeks old and my parents were on their way to the Cleveland Clinic to have Daddy's arteries roto-rootered. Dad was so sick that he was unable to get out of the car once they arrived. So I opened the door and held Billy up so Daddy could touch his face.

The Cleveland Clinic, by the way, worked wonders on his ailing heart. They sent him back home with renewed energy. But his liver and kidneys were still misbehaving, and there wasn't much anyone could do about that. Daddy started going in and out of the hospital around this time, which wore my mother out.

He could not—would not—stay there alone, so Mom spent 12 hours a day there too. As soon as she got home, she said, the phone would be ringing. Most of the time, it was Daddy barking orders about what he wanted or needed for the next day. Other times it was some angry nurse, complaining about something he'd done. One called to plead with my mother to stop my father from taking his monitors off and leaving the ward. "Every time he does that," she said, "it sets off an alarm."

So there I was, a mother to an unhappy someone else without ready access to mine. I was sleeping three or four hours a night at best. My husband started calling me "the night stalker." Three of my four stepsons were still at home, and I was still the family's primary bread-winner.

My obstetrician called me once to discuss my mood. "I did not like what I saw when you came to my office," she said. "Your lack of affect concerns me." She suggested that I might want to see somebody about it, but I blew her off. I'd spent a whole lot of my life feeling lousy. It was nothing new to me. I knew how to muddle through and get things done—after all, I'd been through worse.

I kept getting up and going to work. I kept taking care of Billy. By then I had mastered the art of emotional reassignment and had learned to get through one negative thing at a time. I was a master at giving my concerns voice by then—something my husband found very disturbing. "You know you talk to yourself like you have someone with you?" he once said.

My response to him was "And ... ?"

By this stage of my life I had all my weaknesses in full view, and I knew when I was entertaining them. I would write down my thoughts and read through them regularly so I could see when I was about to make a left turn. I had also become very adept at working in opposition to how I felt.

When a moment of real crisis arose, I'd call Mom. We'd talk it out and I'd get through it. I was flying low, but I was level. No one was going to crash. I was on my way to making something workable out of it when the very last thing someone would have picked for me to do became my next move. After eighteen years, the municipal judge in my city retired, and I decided to run for office.

Billy was around 10 months old. He had just started to walk. The courthouse was just blocks from my house, and judges set their own schedule. The heads of the local Republican Party said they'd back me if I decided to run for the job. In my state of sleep-deprived delirium, I thought I saw the hand of God at work. An answer to my prayers, I reasoned. I started to campaign.

This, Mom said, waylaid Daddy once again; his death, once more, had to be put on hold. This time, though, Daddy seemed really excited about sticking around. The thought of his little girl becoming a judge set a fire under him that none of us had seen in a while. He helped me raise money, gave a lot of his own, and called often to give advice. All of his friends told him, "Don't get too excited, Bill, she can't win," which is exactly the kind of stuff he likes to hear.

I too, heard a number of predictions that all ended with me getting murdered at the polls. Even the guy who talked me into doing it said I couldn't win. Objectively, all of the nay-sayers were right. I was only 33 years old. I was working full-time and had a ten-month-old baby on my hands. I had no political base, no experience, and no sense of humor at all.

Had I been getting more sleep, I might have seen it as a lost cause. But luckily, I was a little punchy and really thought I had a chance. Good thing, too, because this is where my misfortune—and my mother's rules—combined to help me beat the odds. I took what I learned while swirling the drain and rode it right into court.

Because I have spent so much of my life standing out in left field, popular wisdom has never meant much to me at all. So what everyone else was saying didn't give me a moment's pause. Nor did I do the things the powers-that-be said that I should do, like going to local officials for endorsements and ring-kissing. This too, I now realize, was a good thing, since I firmly believe that following the traditional wisdom would have gotten me a traditional ass-whupping. My best bet was to conduct my campaign from left field, a place where I felt more comfortable.

Though I showed up at all of the candidates' forums to plead for endorsements I knew I wouldn't get, I did not go to any of the local politicians to kiss their rings or look for an inside track. They told me not to concentrate too much on black voters, because they were the least likely to come to the polls. So that's all I did—except I showed up at their houses three or four times to drive the point home. When the local newspaper called us in to get our opinions on things, all of the candidates went into their standard political spiel when they were asked a specific question. I, however, answered his precise inquiry with equal precision, preceded by the following statement: "I might be showing my political naiveté, but I plan on answering the questioned that you asked." I guess the guy liked my answer because I got the endorsement, my youth and inexperience notwithstanding.

I took this left-field approach and combined it with Rule Number 5: No Matter What, Keep Coming. I logged a lot of miles knocking on neighbors' doors. I then used Rule Number 10(B)4: Take it To Another Level to help me with my shyness. I had a hard time going door-to-door, so I pretended I was doing something else. I made a game out of it. I made bets about who would be home, their gender, and their color. I counted steps in between doors so I could feel good about the exercise I was getting. I also used Rule Number 10 (B) and enlisted my husband's assistance. He found campaigning fun and invigorating rather than daunting. I told the man to push me when I started to slow down. I also used Rule Number 9 and got my mind right about his pushy attitude when he started getting on my nerves.

Last, but not least, I used my ability to speak to my advantage. Politicians always seem to say what they are going to say no matter who they are with. But I listened more than I spoke, so I could figure out just how it was my audience wanted to feel. Then I would phrase the truth as I saw it in a manner in which they could hear it. I can be, as a result, a very effective public speaker, and I swayed many people that way.

Difficulties teach. Attempts to rise above them strengthen. I took what wasn't working well for me and made it into a weapon, and I won. Not by much, mind you. Six votes was my margin of victory. But a win is a win, and I took the bench ready to set the world afire. Of course, that didn't happen, but I gave it my best shot.

THE RULES

The Act of Balancing

In the end, it is all about balance. If you are looking for *the answer* to anything, you have landed in the wrong universe. It's all about knowing what to do with each problem that you have. Sometimes Approach A will work. Sometimes it's Approach B. Other times you have to take a bit of both to come up with your own Approach C. In order to do that, though, you have to overcome your emotional desire for certainty. One must learn to live easily with words like "maybe," "sometimes," and "could be."

RULE NUMBER 22: The All-Ramifications Rule

Nothing is ever all good or all bad. Good things carried too far can become a problem. Likewise, bad stuff, if responded to appropriately, can strengthen and teach you better than all of the instruction in the world.

With this in mind, you have to keep a cautious eye on the good things in your life to make sure they stay good, while making a conscious effort to find a constructive way to make use of the bad things.

Case in Point: In 1964, my sister and I were the only two black kids in an all-white, lower-middle-class elementary school. "It ain't a cigar but a niggar," is the phrase my sister always recites when asked about those days. I, on the other hand, remember standing in front of Towers Court South Pool, looking through the gate my sister and I were forbidden to enter and watching our white classmates frolicking in the water.

We went home and told Daddy, who found out that it was a private pool and as such could deny entrance to anyone its operators pleased. A month or so later, my sister and I found ourselves at the downtown Columbus YMCA, a place frequented primarily by urban blacks, and that's where we learned to swim. We also learned what a "rich-bitch motherfucker" was at the Y. It seems our long hair and relative affluence made us outsiders there as well.

So there we were, niggers on one side of town and rich bitches on the other. Result? There are very few places that I can go where I feel uncomfortable because of who I am. Years later, when I began working, I encountered the following demographic statistics at my firm:

Number of lawyers: around 200.
Number of black lawyers: 6.
Number of black female lawyers: me.

And you know what? I hardly noticed. It didn't bother me at all. Reaping the rewards of the rougher road, I felt right at home. James Road Elementary had prepared me well, it removed a whole layer of 'other anxiety' that often gives people fits.

RULE NUMBER 23: Know When to Holler for Help

Just as the All-Ramifications Rule requires that you should never label anything as all good or all bad, so it is with experts. The thing is that you have to understand what they are for and not believe everything they say. Their words, thoughts, and advice must be examined just like anything else. They are human too, despite the many letters strung behind their names; they have odd points of view, predilections, and biases, just like anyone else. But if used correctly and with constant vigilance, they can really help you out.

Case in Point: As I wrote earlier, I fell down in 1996, just tripped and plopped flat on my face. I was the mother of two by then and in my second year on the bench. I was the president of the local chapter of a national organization called The Links and on the boards of a number of organizations. I had it all handled (or at least, I thought so), but after a while, I simply unraveled. I don't exactly know what it was, but I became anxious, angry, unhappy, and morose.

I parceled out the few periods of clarity I had two hours at a time. Using every emotional management skill that I had, I made sure that I stayed calm and focused on the bench. Likewise, when I was dealing directly with the boys, I would marshal a sense of purpose around me so they wouldn't see me fly apart. I distinctly remember saying to myself, out loud and quite often, "You know it isn't them." That was the mantra I used to focus past my upset so I wouldn't upset them.

My mother came up for an unexpected visit. I think my husband had made a call. Neither one will admit to it, but I believe that's exactly what happened. Mom watched me for a couple a days and then we sat down to talk. Ever so gently, she suggested that it might be time for me to holler for help.

Though my obstetrician had suggested the same thing months earlier, this time it made sense to me. My mother has a way of putting things that anticipates and negates all opposition before I can even think about saying no.

So off I went to a psychologist. We talked for a while. I took a long, drawn-out test. He then scheduled me for a return appointment. "What nonsense," I thought as I left his office, feeling every bit as badly as I did when I went in.

I went back the next week, and when he told me what was wrong, I had the nerve to express disbelief.

"Depressed?" I repeated incredulously.

"No, '*severely* depressed,'" was his response.

He sent me directly to my doctor. He gave me something to take.

"Good move," my sister said. "You'll like Zoloft, it will even you out."

No truer words were ever spoken. The next year of my life was the easiest I can remember. After a couple of weeks, the Zoloft took away the feeling that I was walking on the razor's edge. I did not have to fight so hard to maintain control; steady was no longer such a struggle. Though to the outside world I still behaved the same (no one but my mother, sister, and husband could tell the difference), being calm and cool now came much more naturally.

I believe my year of living easily was a great affirmation of my mother's rules. My time on Zoloft demonstrated that by following her rules, I had learned to behave reasonably and rationally even though it was contrary to my nature; it was then I truly understood the value of what I knew.

Nine

What a Little Crazy Will Do For You

Have you ever looked around and wondered how you got where you are? I mean, is your life just as you expected it to be? Or are you more than just a bit surprised by how things have turned out?

I think about that kind of thing a lot. My life continues to surprise me. As an accidental overachiever who never planned to do the things I've done, I am here despite my best efforts to get other places that are not quite as good. Since a little money and a lot of solitude was all I ever wanted, I've often wondered, how in the world did things turn out like this?

I mentioned it to my mother once.

"I know what you mean," she said. "Who would have thought that someone as odd as you would turn out quite so well?"

Certainly not me, that's for sure, but for reasons most don't understand. While I am grateful for my unexpected life with all of its unearned rewards, neither being a judge nor appearing on a TV show make me feel "successful." In fact, the achievement I'm most proud of did not involve notoriety of any kind. My most treasured triumph was conveyed in comment, and it only took four words.

One day, my mother came to my court and watched me sentence people. When I finished, we went back into my chambers and she said, "You have them, too."

"What?" I asked, rather distracted. Sentencing days were always busy.

"Your Second Set of Eyes. You look past what people are telling you and see what's really going on."

I could have received no better accolade. Her belief in me spoke volumes. What could be better than knowing that the person you admire most now thinks you can do what she does best?

I think I was a good judge—not a great one, but definitely good. Generally solid, occasionally inspired, but always trying something new in an effort to do better. And I believe I was good because, and not in spite of, the things I have been through.

Take for instance, the stranger factor, the thing that makes people instinctively dislike the unfamiliar. Prejudice, bias, whatever you want to call it—we are all subject to that kind of thinking. But if you ask most judges if they're biased, they'll say absolutely not. I know because I used to teach judicial education courses, and that's what they told me when I asked. Now don't get me wrong. I don't blame them. What else could a judge say? After all, the rules *require* them to say it. Besides, can you imagine what the public would do with a judge who admitted to being prejudiced? The truth of the statement notwithstanding, that would be the last he saw of his job.

The problem is that too many judges actually *believe* what the world forces them to say. This is a violation of Rule Number 18, which prohibits believing the lies you tell other people. It is a common mistake, which doesn't make it any less dangerous. Everyone owns an odd point of view and the occasional howling bias. There is no getting away from it, even if it isn't what you intend, since prejudice has more to do with how you feel than what you think. The fact that we judges rarely acknowledge it only makes it worse. You can't minimize or manage a bias you don't admit to having.

Compliments of the rougher road, I have tried to learn how to minimize the harm my own humanity can cause. I have spent a lifetime setting aside what I feel and picking it apart. I know good and well that I will never *really* be impartial, no matter how hard I try, and I believe that understanding this allows me to be more impartial than most. Having honed my emotional management skills, second-guessing my first reaction is second nature to me now. I never believe what I *think* with out taking a good look at what I *feel*. That way, I am better able to see a bias coming.

Being a good judge, however, requires much more than controlling your biases. A good judge can never get too comfortable. A judge always has the last word on any given day, whether it is right or wrong. I, however, have my very own private peanut gallery, my very own judge and jury, thanks to my Beast, that big, ugly bitch that follows me around whispering, "Is this right?" and "Are you sure?" She holds me to a standard of conduct I know I'll never meet. When I act out of something more than the purest of motives, she'll keep me up at night muttering, "What have you done?" In her never-ending search for the worst in what I do, the Beast will not allow me to hold on to an opinion simply because it's mine. Since she is always looking for flaws in my reasoning, I can't get married to my ideas. Once an imperfection is revealed, she makes me get next to the better one.

And then there is the worst of judicial ailments—the Black Robe Disease, which is otherwise known as arrogance.

Picture this. Your place is at the front of the room on an elevated bench. As you enter, everyone else must rise. Court may have been scheduled to begin an hour or so ago, but as everyone knows, the start time you set applies to everyone but you. You take your seat, and then everyone else may. Your bailiff leans over and whispers a thing or two; you look around; she calls the first case, and from then on, everybody in your airspace does exactly as they are told. You sit there for an hour or two, and depending on exactly what kind of judge you are, you spend that time putting people in jail, separating children from their mothers, or taking large sums of money from one guy and giving it to another. You might also get to tell a man where he will spend the rest of his life or, more alarming yet, have the opportunity to set a date for him to lose it.

Of course, if you are a municipal judge, like I was, you don't have that much authority. But you still get to do a whole lot of stuff regular people can't. You can put people out of their homes; you can send a sheriff into their houses and auction off their personal property. You can sign a paper that allows the police to burst into their houses and look for stuff they don't want anybody to know they have. And yes, you can put people in jail. Not for long, mind you, but they still have to go just because you said so.

No matter what kind of judge you are, if you have been on the bench for a while, you are now working with people who have learned your likes and dislikes and have begun to cater to them. No one interrupts you, and everyone apologizes to you a lot even when you're the one who's wrong. And as if that isn't enough, you have at your disposal the *piece de resistance* of authority: the ability to summarily incarcerate those who fail to show you the proper respect.

Now tell me something: do you feel it yet, that sense of power and control; that feeling that something must be special about you?

Not many judges will ever tell you how seductive their job is. When asked, most say that they are honored and humbled by the opportunity to serve, and they emphasize the sense of responsibility it gives them. They will not, however, tell you about the rush they got the first time they donned that robe and sat up in that big leather chair. Or how satisfying it feels to shut down some arrogant lawyer or to jail the local idiot whose conduct you find so offensive. Power is a potent drug with great addictive potential.

Fortunately, my Beast has a very hard time catching a buzz. Though I am not immune from arrogance, it is hard for me to sustain. My Beast simply does not believe in my ability. She thinks I have only fooled the world. She laughs when I feel accomplished. She never lets me feel too good for too long. "Soon the world will know you for what you really are," she says, "It's only a matter of time."

Even if the Beast just up and walked away one day, I would still be held to earth by my vivid memories. I will never be able to take myself too seriously because I know what a fool I used to be. I wanted to live in a closet, for God's sake. It's hard to forget that kind of thing.

Finally, there is one last disease known to afflict judges; its primary symptom is a pronounced lethargy that grows as the years go by. Most judges can easily work the job so they don't have to work very hard. I had the busiest municipal court docket in the state, if you look at it on a judge-per-case basis, and I was still able to make a short day of it most of the time without slowing down the process. Any judge expending any effort at all can manage to do the same thing. Many do much worse.

Fortunately, I was unable to carry that kind of thing too far, for the idle mind is, indeed, the playground of my particular beastly devil. So in order to keep from losing my mind, I thought up things to do—ones that went beyond the basics and, I hope, might have done some good.

I ran a program for at-risk teenage girls, and then another for the boys. I had a traveling road show that I took to local fourth-grade students that allowed them to act out the things they needed to know about the judicial system in order to pass the fourth-grade proficiency exam. I also got local judges together to discuss the issue of the mentally ill in court. I did videotapes to help people who came to court without a lawyer, which were designed to walk them through the judicial process. I designed and wrote a newsletter so folks knew what was going on in court. You name it, I did it—all for free and without paying others to assist me.

The greatest gift of my early life was my ability to make myself understood. I learned to talk a good game on Weyant Avenue. I learned to read Daddy and his responses to the things people said. That way I was better able to get through to him when he was not all there. I have a better fix now on what I did instinctively when I was a kid. I looked past what was going on in the house and focused on what was happening in his head. I developed my ability to listen in order to understand people's emotions and needs. Meanwhile, I had taught myself to set aside whatever I was feeling so I could concentrate on the task at hand.

I learned this is quite a handy ability to have, especially when you spend your days trying to convince all manner of people to change the way they look at things. Incarceration without elucidation is a waste of time. If a guy goes to jail thinking, "That judge is a bitch," he's no better for the experience. But if he goes to jail thinking she might have a point, some growth or enlightenment may actually occur.

In return, I was met by the occasional victory. One young man stopped me in the street to thank me for what I had done for him.

Once while in the grocery store, a young lady came up to me with a two- or three-year-old girl in tow. She said, "I know you don't remember me but I was in your court two years ago. She was just a baby then," she pointed to her daughter, "and my boyfriend was in on a domestic violence charge, and I just wanted to say thank you. You talked to both of us for a long time and you gave me some real good advice. Things aren't perfect but they're a whole lot better and I wanted to thank you for that."

In fact, I tend to get a great deal of love in the grocery store. That's where I run into people who have run into me in court. By far the thing I hear the most is that they appreciated the time I took to talk to them, and though they didn't see it at the time, my words made sense to them now.

So I know exactly what a little crazy has done for me. It has made me think and feel in a way that helps me in what I do. Having developed, as my mother says, my Second Set of Eyes, I can better see the emotional currents that capsize my clientele's boats. This, in turn, has allowed me to witness what I think are the most common emotional mistakes people make, and to formulate responses to them. These are what I hope to address in the rest of this book.

THE RULES

The Rules of Persuasion

My mother is a master at getting her point across not because she is eloquent, but because she knows how to read people. I have tried to use that knowledge to my advantage, and it was the most useful knowledge I ever took to the bench.

RULE NUMBER 24: Understand Your Audience

Often your ability to persuade has little to do with the rationality of your argument. Emotions, more than logic, dictate what people hear and believe. So you have to understand what your audience is feeling before you can get your audience to understand you.

To do this, you must first understand what it is *you* are feeling—and then set those feelings aside. You can't hear what someone is saying if you are busy, say, defending yourself, being insulted, or just standing there, disgusted. So step back and pretend you are eavesdropping on two other peoples' conversation. Listen simply to understand. People—all people—can be fascinating if you look at them the way a researcher would. So make a habit of getting a little more clinical in your observations as you knock about the world. Pay attention as if you were collecting data.

Once you have gotten yourself out of the way, you must listen past the topic at hand. The other guy's frustration, fear, or anger will almost always trump his logic. Look for those things first and try to understand how the issue of the moment implicates them. Once you figure that out, it will help you address the pertinent concerns.

Case in Point: I had a domestic violence case once in which a mother was brought in for pouncing on her husband in the midst of an argument about their sixteen-year-old son's academic crash-and-burn. Pop wanted to enlist outside help. Mom countered with arguments involving time and money. Neither party wanted to be in court. Their son had called the police. So the husband came to me to plead for lenience and explain the situation. When he did, the two of them stood right in front of me and started debating test-prep services again. I listened and watched for a while so I could figure out how to redefine their difficulties for them before I sent them home.

After a while, it became eminently clear why they couldn't resolve their problem. When Pop said "tutoring help," Mom heard "Doris, you're a failure as a mom." She calmed down a bit when I told her of the academic drama in my own home and all the help my son was getting. "You know," I said, "I was feeling like an utter failure at my house until I found my son the right help. Sometimes it's not about how hard you try or what you know, it's about what you are willing to do."

Of course, this woman did not all of a sudden see the light and acquiesce. But she did start to listen and that's always the first step to understanding.

RULE NUMBER 25: Wait Until They're Ready

When it comes to persuasion, timing is a very important factor that people tend to overlook. Anger does little to clear your head, increase your vocabulary, or enhance your ability to speak. If you discuss something of importance while the parties involved are angry, you will not be able to get your point across. The yeller can't express himself well, and the yellee is too busy defending himself to be able to absorb and understand.

Sometimes, all it takes to win an argument is to bring the issue up at a time when the wrong emotions won't get in the way. Never underestimate the value of a good meal, or a little well-timed sex. If your husband, say, is currently feeling good about you, he is more likely to feel good about what you have to say.

Case in Point: My mother never bothered to argue with my father when he was Unhinged. You cannot reason with a disease.

Worse yet, if she had gotten all excited when talking to him, it would have made him even angrier.

She would not, however, let issues she needed to address go unattended. Instead, she stored the issue away without ruminating on it, so it wouldn't bring down her mood. Then, on the right day, Mom would bring it up. Gently, and without animosity, she would make her position known.

This rule works even better with people who are *not* psychotic. I use it with my husband all of the time. For instance, he used to show up late a lot. It drove me out of my mind. For years, I'd express my dismay as soon as he showed up, mistakenly believing that as long as I wasn't yelling I was being heard. And I could not understand, for the life of me, why things weren't getting better.

When informed of my difficulty, my mother said, "Don't complain when he shows up late, just get in the car and go. If you start in on him then he'll see you, and not his tardiness, as the biggest problem that he has.

"Wait until you are having a good day and then say something like, 'I don't know what it is about me, but late just makes me crazy. I know it might be tough for you, but can you work with it?'"

I followed my mother's advice and sure enough, it worked. Once I rephrased the problem and brought it up in a time of relative calm, my husband began to see showing up on time as doing me a favor, instead of dealing with a conflict. This removed a whole level of emotional resistance and helped him focus on the logistics of getting where he needed to be when he needed to be there. And, slowly but surely, he started showing up closer and closer to on time.

RULE NUMBER 26: Start Where Other People Are and Slowly Walk Them Home

You can't get people to change their minds by telling them that they're wrong. There is no designated decibel level at which sound waves will dislodge a person's errant ideas. Moreover, people simply hate to change, and they don't much like to admit that they're wrong, either. A successful emotional approach to persuasion must take all of this into account.

When arguing, most people focus on the weaknesses in the other guy's position to the exclusion of all else. However, if you do that, the other guy will think you don't understand what he's saying and he'll keep repeating what he's already said.

Remember, there is some level of logic that rests somewhere in most of what anybody says. It may not be good logic, but it still makes sense to the person who says it. In order to be persuasive, you must be able to address your opponent's entire understanding of a situation. Then you must repeat it to him, so he knows you see his point.

Once you've done that, he's more likely to engage you in a productive dialogue, and that's when you gather up all of your courage and give him something he wants. Sometimes it's little more than respect for his position. But whatever it is, a small concession will take the fight-or-flight response down a notch.

Once you've got him listening with less emotional static in the way, start walking him home slowly. People will stand their ground much harder if you ask for too much right away. So tell them where it is they need to be and give them some suggestions on how to get there. The steps should appear small and should contain something in it for them.

Case in Point: John had been charged with assault for hitting his next-door neighbor. They had been feuding about some nonsense for months, and he'd finally had enough.

He pled guilty, and while I was sentencing him, something became very clear. John thought of himself as the victim. His neighbor was pushy, ridiculous, and irritating (I know, because he came to court). He was a meticulous, relentless man who could let no small matter rest.

Believing that even Mother Teresa would have wanted to deck this guy, John saw his trip to court as just one more thing this idiot did to him. He kept telling me over and over again how intractable the situation had become.

From dealing with other provoked assaults, I knew that if I did not address his belief that he had no choice, he wouldn't hear a single word I said. He would have rolled his eyes, pled no contest, and immediately tuned me out.

But since these guys still lived next door to each other, I had to give this man another way to go. So I leaned across the bench and said, "I know just how you felt." Then I described to him how he was feeling and told him I thought it was understandable. From that point on he was listening to me, so I could start walking him my way.

Then I set him up with a road map to another outcome. We walked through what he did with an eye towards other options. I tried to convince him that part of what this other guy was looking for was exactly what he got. He liked taking up other people's time and commanding attention. I told John that disregarding him would eventually register as defeat.

Though I don't know what ultimately happened, I do know that John felt more in control when he left. And in control is what he needed be in order to keep this kind of thing from happening again.

▶ *Ten*

Other People's Errors

One day I told my bailiff that I was going to buy a neon sign that said, "What's wrong with you people?" That way at the appropriate moment—let's say five or six times a day—I could press a button, light up the sign, and then just send everybody to jail. "Quite a time-saver," I suggested, "and it would certainly keep me from having to repeat myself."

Of course, I wasn't serious. They have rules about the dignity of judicial office that frown on that kind of thing. Lack of practicality notwithstanding, the idea helped put things in perspective for me, and allayed some of my more compelling (but less than judicial) urges. Like the occasional impulse I had to smack some poor soul who had no way of knowing that he was the sixth guy that day to say, "Yeah, I hit him, but it wasn't my fault—let me tell you what he said."

These are the defendants who make a judge shake her head and ask, "What in the world were you thinking?" which is, of course, a very silly question since most misdemeanant misbehavior occurs because those involved simply weren't thinking at all.

Why, you might wonder, am I bothering to discuss the people I met in court? What, you might think, do they have to do with you? After all, you have never drop-kicked your neighbor's dog or smacked your grandma with a chair. I contend, however, that while my clientele's problems are somewhat spectacular, they were caused by emotional failures we all engage in regularly. And I believe if we search for ourselves in them (despite the exceptional nature of their troubles), we can profit from costly lessons learned completely free of charge. Based in biology, egged on by society, and often altered by the prevailing view of things, most bad situations start with a few simple emotions that have stood the test of time. As a result, I believe that my clientele's antics are instructive if you pay less attention to "the what" and concentrate on "the why."

The first thing you have to do in order to learn from others' errors is take a good look at the context of our times. Every society has trends, tendencies, and a unique way of doing things. You have to know what river you're swimming in so you can decide whether or not you should swim with or against it.

Americans, for example, have an awful lot of stuff. We live lives of ease, lives people in many other countries can hardly imagine. Food abounds; healthcare, though expensive, is quite good. Things aren't perfect for all of us, but compared to how we lived 50 years ago, Americans live lives of incredible, yet often unrecognized, ease. As a result, we now have the time to get very worked up about stuff that really shouldn't rate: road rage, air rage, parents killing one another at badly officiated hockey games.

Today, too many people rush to court if they don't get their way. They sue everything and everybody when they don't get what they want. Remember that Tennessee school I mentioned, which was threatened with a lawsuit when it posted its honor roll on the wall? In response, the school district decided that no school could post its honor rolls. Another father in New York went to federal court in an effort to get his teenage son's wrestling call overturned. This is just the tip of the iceberg, people.

I watched in amazement from the bench as this tide of tirades swamped my court. I soon realized that a lot of very ordinary people are roaming around out there just one comment away from raising the roof on a completely ordinary situation. One 60-year-old woman came in after having assaulted a woman who ditched her in line. She actually jumped on this woman in the parking lot and hung on to her neck. Another day, I had a whole neighborhood in court when a rude 11-year-old got into it with an immature store clerk. The next thing you know, a whole group of grown men were squaring off with each other in the parking lot.

These kinds of situations are glaringly extreme, but they arise too often to be no more than just individual mistakes. We have, I believe, established a culture of desire and demand that fails to recognize both responsibility and dumb luck. It seems we have a hard time looking in the mirror when we are looking for someone to blame. We have an "it's not my fault" mentality that threatens to render us perpetual quests on Dr. Phil.

When as a society we become used to getting things without maintaining a corresponding sense of responsibility, we end up with a two-year-old's perspective on the world. Everyone begins to believe that the world, most certainly and appropriately, revolves around them. And when you feel that way, when things don't go your way, you feel not just surprised, but insulted.

Now, I'm sure you haven't pounced on someone for ditching you in line. I also doubt you have gotten into a street fight because someone was rude to your kids. However, you still must ask yourself whether this particular affective error is lurking somewhere in your own backyard. You always have to ask yourself: Am I getting carried away by some cultural current of some kind? Are my decisions really mine, or have the moods of those around me told me what to think?

For instance, whenever something goes wrong, do you look first for the mistake *you* made? Or are you more prone to scan for what everyone else did wrong? Do you complain about what's going on to and around you without ever offering an answer?

Of course, other people's errors aren't just about the culture and the time we live in; they are about all of us as individuals and how perceptive and controlled we are. This is, of course not, the kind of thing that will take care of itself. You have to pay attention to your emotional life and how it's shaping who you are. You have to ask yourself, all day long, am I thinking, or am I feeling?

In so doing, you must focus on the real cause of your dismay and how your own perspective may have colored things. Are you carrying extra weight, or extra debt, because you can't walk past the way you feel in order to do what you need to do? Have you said, "One more time won't matter" so often that now, it really does? And what about all of the things you know you ought to be doing but can't seem to get done? Do you have explanations for things left unaccomplished that may not be as reasonable as you try to make them sound?

You must decide to get comfortable with whatever's wrong with you. Have you taken that good look in the bathroom mirror? Or is everybody around you telling you the same thing, but you remain convinced that they're all wrong? Do you believe that the only reason they don't agree with you is because they are not standing in your shoes? And if so, have you considered that the only thing unique about your footwear is the way they make you *feel*?

Ultimately, the question is simply this: how much responsibility do you take for the things that happen to you? In a society that now brings lawsuits to recover for our own decisions as to what we smoke and eat, have you fallen into the false comfort of believing that so much of what ails you is really beyond your control? Or do you simply go with how you feel and think up explanations later? When something unexpected goes wrong, do you wait for the rush to go away before you decide what you should do?

You ought to ask yourself these questions whenever you see other people's lives go awry. Read the stories I offer here about the kinds of people I saw in my courtroom. Even if you do not see yourself when reading about their problems, you should still ask yourself whose life could not be a little better, and a little bit more in control?

For instance, can you work with just about anybody at home or at work? Or does your ability to conduct business depend on the person with whom you're dealing? Are you the cool breeze in a heated situation, or are you the most flammable material there? Are you capable of pulling up the better part of yourself when circumstances demand? Or do you find that the worst of you normally ends up handling the unexpected and unpleasant?

Even beyond handling potentially explosive situations, there is an art to feeling well. Wouldn't you like to avoid experiencing the interpersonal irritations that short of taking up residence in a cave, no one can ever hope to completely avoid? Better yet, wouldn't you like to be able to walk north in a crowd of people running south and not become concerned? Don't you think that alone and okay is something worth working for?

The question is this: How well do you function in a world that, more often than not, does not function well?

In the following chapters, I have categorized some of the more common emotional mistakes that brought people into my court. I will then point out where these people went wrong by violating one of my mother's rules. Afterward, I will supply you with the rules themselves, in hope that you might see a bit of yourself in where my clientele went wrong.

THE RULES

The Commandments of Culture

A culture, like a crowd, has a personality of its own. When we get together, we do things we would never consider doing on our own. Every once in a while, you have to stop and make sure the rising tide of a ridiculous but popularly held opinion is not rising around you. These rules are designed to help you see when that particular dam is about to break.

RULE NUMBER 27: Beware Entitlement Inflation

My mom says you are entitled to very few things: a mother who loves you (although I would say two parents who love you) and an opportunity to reap the benefits of your efforts. Everything else, she claims, are things for which you should be grateful. And while I really do think Mom may have carried this one a bit too far, she still has a point.

People who feel entitled to everything get disappointed a lot.

The problem is that sometimes it is hard to tell the difference between what you are actually owed and what you simply want. In order to avoid confusing the two, you must keep a limited, clearly defined, and specific list of entitlements in your head. That way, the next time you feel abused or misused, you can return to that list and see if the thing you've been denied is on it. If not, it might be best to just get over it.

Now, certainly, you have the right to want things in life, and to be disappointed when you don't get them. But while you are busy getting agitated, always ask yourself these questions: What does the size of the thing that is so upsetting me say about how small I am? And what mountain will fall down around me if I don't get what I want this time?

Case in Point: I read an article in my local paper about a girl whose father took a school district to court because they wouldn't let his daughter on the soccer team. The fact that they missed the sign-up deadline because they were vacationing in Canada was not a consideration. It was the fact that she couldn't have something she really wanted that dictated this man's response.

RULE NUMBER 28: Increase Your Nonsense Threshold

If you look for insult everywhere you go, that's exactly what you'll find.

Judging things and finding fault is basic to human nature. Unfortunately, such judgments can keep you from enjoying new and different things that really can't do you any harm. They also add new items to your worry quotient that really shouldn't rate, thus making your life seem more precarious and beleaguered than it really is. Remember, small things only bother small people.

So relax. Get over it. And realize that sometimes you have to *work* to make it not matter.

Case in Point: Gary Larson, the cartoonist who created "The Far Side," put out several collections of his work, one of which (*The Pre-History of The Far Side: A 10th Anniversary Exhibit*, if you want to get it for yourself) had a whole section on negative responses he'd received to his cartoons he drew. (You would be amazed at how indignant people can manage to get over a cartoon.)

In it, he shared a letter from the Jane Goodall Institute about a cartoon that depicted a gorilla removing a blonde hair from another gorilla. The caption read "Well, well—another blonde hair ... conducting a little more 'research' with that Jane Goodall tramp?"

The Institute which bore Ms. Goodall's name wrote in to express its outrage at Mr. Larson for referring to such a renowned scientist as a "tramp." In it they used the words "atrocity," "inexcusable," "incredibly offensive," and "absolutely stupid."

But while the institution was so busy taking offense, Ms. Goodall herself was simply laughing. She liked it so much she had the cartoon printed on t-shirts that were sold by her institute for fundraising purposes.

RULE NUMBER 29: Watch Your Superlatives

You can talk yourself in and out of all kinds of moods without ever meaning to do it. Listen to yourself some time when you speak and pay attention to the kind of words you use. Examine your working vocabulary for evidence of the extreme. Plow through all your daily commentary for unnecessary value judgments and negative assumptions.

For example, do you use the word "blame" when, in reality, you are only talking "responsibility"? Was the project really "crippled" by someone's failure or was it simply "set back"? Was the incident truly a "tragedy" or just an "unfortunate circumstance"? And what about the word "outrage"? Since when is it an everyday expression that applies to everything?

If you call all misfortune "horrific" and every upset "traumatic," your base emotionality will go up and your tolerance level down. Next thing you know, you will be getting upset over smaller and smaller things.

Case in Point: There was a letter writer in our local newspaper who suggested that people who smoke cigarettes ought to have their children taken away. Now, you really have to ask yourself at some point—is this really the way we want to go?

RULE NUMBER 30: Globalize Your Pain Quotient

This one is simple. You do not live in Afghanistan, or in the drought-ravaged Sudan. And, yes, the lady in front of you has 30 coupons, a personal check (but no check-cashing card), and at least one question about the price of every product in her cart.

Case in Point: One day, while I was standing in the check-out line at the grocery store, I became so visibly agitated that the man behind me tapped me on the shoulder and told me that such delays were just God's way of letting some trouble elsewhere pass you by. "There could be a traffic accident out there," he said, "that He's trying to keep you from."

"How ludicrous," was my initial thought. Mumbling to myself about the masses' ability to believe anything, I dismissed his comment as a testament to his lack of understanding. But as I stood there, becoming increasingly agitated by this circumstance over which I had not control, I watched him out of the corner of my eye. This man, who I'd been mocking in my mind, was calm and relaxed while I was half out of my mind. That's when I realized that, all my educated rationality notwithstanding, this man and I were in the same predicament, but I was the only one who was upset.

And while I was never able to accept his theory, I came up with one of my own. I universalized my pain quotient and pulled up the relevant facts. During the fifteen minutes or so I stood in line to buy food for my kids, there was another mother somewhere holding a starving baby that she loved as much as I did my own. With that, I lost the urge to be angry, picked up an *Enquirer*, and kept myself amused until it was my turn at the register.

Eleven

Somewhere East of Reason

My mother rarely gets angry, but when she does, she usually does so on purpose. Every once in a while she will just "deliver one" to make sure everybody understands that even she has her limits. But more often than not, she simply gets quiet when most others get upset—waiting for, I later learned, the chemical rush of anger to wash away before she makes her next move.

My mother's take on anger is simple: "Once you get mad, you lose." That one took me decades to understand. It took me even longer to conquer. I was 40 before I felt I had really gotten a handle on this particular skill.

Though I don't get angry often, when I do it can result in a ridiculous scene. So much so that at one point, my mother suggested that I might want to do something about it. "Only get angry if it helps," she said. "You have to learn to call on it when you need it and not let it show up whenever it wants to."

This, as you might imagine, is a very hard thing to do. Mad—aka East of Reason—is a place most people get to before they even know they are on their way there. That's why East of Reason is populated primarily by people who don't know it exists. And while, on occasion, people who know it's there do manage to find it, it's almost never home to those who have the most detailed directions to it. That's because getting there depends more on how you travel than where you are trying to go.

Staying away from East of Reason is all about understanding how you get there. Take, for instance, the Express Train to Angry, the mode of transport one well-educated young businessman took on the way to painting "Molly sucks nigger dick" on the side of his girlfriend's house. He boarded that train, as we all tend to do, seeking immediate relief from the chemical rush that told him he was in danger. His heart hurt, and his manhood felt threatened by his girlfriend's failure to leave all of her affection at home. He rode the fight-or-flight anger rush right into my courtroom.

Several fathers of newly testosteroned sons rode this train to court as well. Once or twice a year I'd see them, and their stories were pretty much the same. Seventeen and sullen, Junior tells his dad he's not taking orders anymore. Unemployed, out of school, and no money notwithstanding, Junior announces to his over-worked father that he is now a man. Next thing you know, one man to another, Junior gets knocked to the floor.

It goes without saying that neither the man whose girlfriend was running around nor the fathers of the obnoxious teens were criminals. They were just regular people who broke the law be-cause they violated my mother's rules. They got caught off guard because they had not, in times of calm, made plans for dealing with predicable triggers. Nor had they learned to recognize what it feels like when the Express Train to Angry is pulling out of the station.

Of course, people don't always get to East of Reason on the ex-press. Sometimes they show up after a very slow ride that's made a whole lot of stops. That's how Diana got there. She'd had a couple of rough weeks. All kinds of things had been going wrong for quite a while. Then, the very last thing she needed to happen did.

Diana was on her way to work one day when her car refused to start. She got a ride to work from a friend, and once she got there, she went straight to her supervisor's office. Informing him of her lat-est mishap, Diana asked for the day off to take her car to the shop. Unsympathetic, her boss said no, and the next thing you know, he was ducking behind his desk trying to avoid a flying stapler.

Once she was in court, I found that Diana's problems were nei-ther uncommon nor particularly big. Instead, I learned that it was the timing that had done her in. Her problems had come so close together that she hadn't taken the time to separate them out. All of the money she didn't have ran headlong into the kids she couldn't control; they, in turn, climbed into the car she was unable to start, and all of it was aimed straight at her unsympathetic boss's head.

A similar emotional mistake brought Joan into court. Due to a series of romantic errors, Joan found herself in the parking lot that day, surrounded by two more mouths than she had the ability to feed and one more on the way. Pregnant and alone, again, her most recent mistake in judgment, Mike, was now refusing to return her calls. Then, as luck would have it, Joan sees Mike's new girlfriend putting packages in her car. Unable to separate her long-term pressures from her immediate concern, she leaped on that woman with all the force of ten years' worth of bad decisions.

Both Diana and Joan ended up places they had no intention of being because they failed to consciously handle their emotional business along the way. My mother made it her business to put a period on things. "Now, let's forget that," is, in fact, one of my mother's favorite phrases. It is how she gives voice to her deliberate decision to end unproductive thought. When she says it she usually crosses her arms, then pulls them apart like an umpire calling safe. My mother believes that every small upset that befalls you must be emotionally identified, separated, and then put away. That way you won't end up East of Reason after traversing the field in which the very last straw is grown.

Although the East of Reason occupants I've discussed so far all got there in different ways, they share one common trait. They were only visitors—renters, so to speak. They got there quickly but didn't stay long. They left when the first rush subsided. However, East of Reason has a number of long-term residents, people who stroll in, wander around for a while, and can't find their way back out.

When I think of those long-term residents, divorcing couples most often come mind. Though both claim that they would like nothing more than to get rid of the other one, they end up buying homes right next door to each other on Balance the Books Boulevard, where nothing is more important than getting even with your neighbor. There, every painful word and unkind gesture must be repaid with interest. Moving on becomes impossible because both parties have so much invested in their new home.

One local architect and his soon-to-be ex-wife were living on that street when he found himself leading the police on a merry chase through a local cemetery with his 3-year-old twins in the back seat. "My day to pick them up from school," he explained. "Her mother got it wrong. And no, I didn't see the five police cars with lights and sirens following me. Oh, and the cemetery thing? It was just a short cut."

Later, his wife filed a lawsuit trying to get compensated for things that have nothing to do with the law. He responded by filing a countersuit for something even sillier. Every time they came to the counter, my clerks scattered, because each filing came with long rants and requests for sympathy. We collected a lot of filing fees and fines from these two people. After a while, they moved on to a higher court because they were now engaging in felonies and suing for amounts too large for a municipal court to award.

Love lost, however, is not the only thing that creates long-term East of Reason residency. Love never returned also prompts a number of people to move in. The Streetcar Named Desire routinely picks up the unaware at the Terminal of Unrequited Love. And if its passengers aren't careful, this particular trolley will transport them all the way to court.

Desire often moves so fast it distorts what those aboard both see and hear. Its riders *want* so desperately that they think they *feel* the truth. That's how, "I don't want to see you anymore" becomes, "I don't want to see you anymore today, but tomorrow could be different," an audio anomaly that authored a number of people's appearances in my court.

Trespassing and telephone-harassment charges often brought the lovelorn to the bench, indictments which were enough to end their flights of fancy. There is, after all, no mistaking an arrest warrant for an invitation to dinner. Of course, those unaffected by such proceedings go on to violate other laws. But they are not the topic of this discussion. No longer East of Reason residents—they've moved to higher elevations where the air is very thin.

We're only concerned with East of Reason here, just beyond the borders of common sense. A place, I contend, any one of us can reach under the right circumstances. You do not have to be out of your mind to get there; all you have to be is upset. That's what the Angry Amendments are for. If employed correctly, they will keep you from making the one critical error that all East of Reason residents ultimately make: believing that their anger is an inescapable consequence of someone else's wrong.

In court, my East of Reasonites almost all identified their conduct as something they could not control. They told me, "It couldn't be helped." They suggested that I would have done the very same thing if I were in their shoes. In fact, most were so convinced of the overwhelming nature of the impetus involved that they suggest that mere knowledge of the circumstances would compel me to find them not guilty.

This, however, never happened, because I understood the rules. Whether you are a stay-at-home mom caught in the whirlwind of taking care of everyone you know, or a corporate executive fighting for money, power, and privilege, it all comes down to the same thing. Do you know what to do with the physiology of rage when you start to feel it? Can you ride out the burn and bother your body manufactures long enough to weigh the whys and wherefores?

More importantly, are you aware of the things that tend to upset you most so you can steel yourself against them? And last but not least, do you regularly test the waters underneath your emotional boat? Are you always aware of how high the swells have grown so some small thing won't swamp your ship?

THE RULES

The Anger Avoidance Amendments

RULE NUMBER 31: The First-Wave Rule

This rule requires you to let the first wave pass you by. The next time you start to feel afraid or angry when no immediate physical threat is present, you must condition yourself to do *nothing*, for at least a second or two.

You'll have to practice. Start the next time you find yourself getting angry. Make a point of isolating and feeling each part of your anger's physical aspects. Note the rapid heartbeat, the warming face, and the sudden desire to act. Stop and purposefully experience each and every part of if it.

While you're doing that, think about how interesting the whole process is in an objective and detached way. Move away from the cause and immerse yourself in the physiology of the response. This inventory, as silly as it sounds, serves two purposes. First, it will help you recognize the storm the next time it comes around.

The second purpose is simply buying time. There is nothing quite as important as placing a moment of rationality between what you *feel* and what you *do*.

Case in Point: I used to get very angry, and when I did I'd quickly lose my sense of proportion. And though I'm too small to hurt anyone with a physical attack, I am, nevertheless, able to do a lot of damage with a barrage of words.

Having honed my Second Set of Eyes at a fairly young age, I've always been able to find the one thing that could hurt a person most. Then, much like a heat-seeking missile, I'd take aim and blow the whole situation apart.

I am proud to say that I do not own that wellspring of anger any more. But when I did, it was clear that I needed to find a way to curb my proclivities before somebody knocked me out.

Mom was the one who noticed it first, the tell-tale phrases I typically used before I'd fall off the rational wagon. Ones like "Let me explain something to you ..." and "You know what your problem is ..." She sat me down and told me about it one day, and then highlighted all of the problems I ran into after I said those kinds of things.

So we decided that if I uttered either one of these phrases, I then had to stop talking altogether. Just sit down, or better yet, call her so I could buy some time. Initially, I unnerved an individual or two when, in the early days of my struggle, I'd fall into an abrupt silence in the middle of an animated conversation. But I stuck to my game plan and eventually learned to keep my responses under control.

RULE NUMBER 32: Beware the Rationale of the Right Now

The Rationale of the Right Now is the fastest road to happy. It's when you fail to consider long-term consequences and decide to go with the flow. The Rationale of the Right Now is a bow to immediacy and only recognizes desire. It's what you engage in when you don't really know what's wrong, but want to feel better right away.

The problem is, the right thing often has the wrong feel to it, and the wrong thing regularly feels good. The fastest road to feeling better is, therefore, usually not the way to go.

This rule asks you to accept that discomfort is a part of life. If you do not expect to feel good all of the time, it will be easier for you to focus beyond your frustration and address the problem at hand.

So get comfortable with your discomfort. Accept that on occasion you'll be displeased, annoyed, unhappy, or otherwise upset. That way you can avoid responding emotionally to a logistical concern.

Case in Point: Take Jane, for instance, a concerned parent who was charged with menacing after threatening her son's teacher with an "ass whuppin" right in front of his entire fourth-grade class. Jane's problems all started the day before, when her son was suspended for fighting. The news of her son's actions and subsequent fate did not sit well with Jane, so with an equally whipped-up relative in tow, Jane came to school to "discuss" the problem, and things got a little out of hand.

Amazed by this woman's level of ire at a seemingly appropriate disciplinary act, I asked Jane, while I was sentencing her, why she had become so upset.

"He has ADD," she explained rather indignantly, "and a suspension is not an appropriate response when an ADD kid acts out." Furious, she expounded, at some length, on the teacher's outrageous conduct. Her voice was tense, her gestures strong. She was genuinely and deeply aggrieved.

Jane violated the First Wave Rule, and then immediately followed up by breaking this one. She was angry, and angry means sit—nothing more or less. Instead, she took the fastest road to happy, which led her straight to court by way of her son's school.

In order to live a well-ordered life, it's imperative to obey the rule regarding The Rationale of the Right Now. It provides that the revelation, "I am angry" should never be followed by the question, "What do I do now?" It further holds that under no circumstance should "I'm upset" directly precede the statement, "Let's go."

RULE NUMBER 33: Don't Let Your Emotions Straddle Events

A lot goes on physiologically when we get afraid and angry. Once the fear chemicals are turned on, they are difficult to turn off, and our bodies don't keep close tabs on what they were dispensed to handle.

So whenever something gets you worked up, make sure you talk yourself down from that agitated state before you move on to something else. Give Voice (see Rule Number 10) to each upsetting occurrence as it happens. Then tell yourself, out loud, that you won't let it bleed into the rest of your life. Intersperse elevating events among your tragedies, in adherence with Rule Number 41. The worse things get, the more important it is to show a passion for the proper things.

Case in Point: I honed this particular rule in court as a means to shift from case to case. On Tuesday mornings I arraigned people. That means I asked them to make a plea to the charges made against them. Often people pled guilty right there and we would then talk about what they did. "Yeah, I hit her, and no, I don't pay child support." I often heard this kind of thing.

Sometimes I became quite strident in my response in order to get a defendant's attention. But when the case was over I'd have to go on to the next, all calm, cool, and collected. Nobody likes to be the next person before a judge after she has just let somebody have it. So I made a point of flashing the next man up a big smile and saying, "Don't worry, I'm not angry. I'm just doing my job, and part of my job is to address each person independently and on his own terms." Not only did this reassure my next defendant, but it also helped me compartmentalize my anger and not let it spill over onto the next guy.

RULE NUMBER 34: Make Sure You Know Where the Mad's Supposed to Go

Since your body has no way of knowing why it's all worked up, angry often ends up going places it has no business being. Typically, misplaced anger falls on the first available target, or the easiest kill. While your body wants to feel better, it doesn't want to get hurt.

So before acting on any anger, you must consider and eliminate all people whose only fault is weakness or proximity. Understand that this is what tends to happen and keep an eye out for it.

Case in Point: I went 30 years without ever suffering from PMS. Peri-menopause changed that, though. Once every six weeks or so, my hormones ran amok. The first few times it happened, my husband took the boys and left the house.

Since I had no idea what was wrong with me, I really thought my husband was being the complete ass that I perceived him to be. After a while, however, I began to notice a pattern to my distress. "Too much angry in too small a space; could it really be him?" I asked myself. "Or is there a better explanation?"

In accordance with the Bathroom Mirror Mandate, I sat down and thought it through. I calculated dates, reviewed complaints, and then I asked myself why. Realizing that my husband's behavior was really no different than it had been before, I came to the only conclusion available. The problem had to be me.

So now I know that on occasion I will rise up from bed in the morning like the bitch from the black lagoon. I accept that everything will irritate me and I vow to suck it up. "This is not to be acted on," I say out loud. "I will not pass this thing along."

I then warn my husband. I don't want to catch him unaware. He needs to know to tread lightly—all emotional hands must be on deck.

And, of course, if none of that works, I buy myself a chocolate cake.

RULE NUMBER 35: The Percentage Rule

Balance is the crux of this particular rule. It's about time, attention, and the ability to prioritize. This rule says everything you do must stay in proper proportion, and that sometimes you have to double-check how you are spending your time.

In order to remain in compliance with this rule, all you have to do is step back, on occasion, and do a priority check. List the things you're doing and how much time they're taking up. Then ask yourself: what was the point of the whole thing when you started out? And did that somehow get lost in the process of getting the thing done?

Case in Point: There was a guy I saw in my courtroom regularly for my first two or three years on the bench. He was an intelligent man with a house and a job and a generally orderly life. Somehow, though, this man got all tied up in the traffic code. Having decided to treat the posted speed limits as mere suggestions, he contended that each person's ability to drive must be taken into account in determining what his speed limit should be. He was so convinced of his position that he began demanding jury trials, believing the average citizen to be equally outraged by this affront.

Of course they didn't see it that way. The jury was picked from residents in the city in which he sought to speed. They were regular citizens with children and they did not want anyone traversing their neighborhood at breakneck speed. So they found him guilty. And instead of having to pay a $55 ticket, the guy got stuck with

$750 in jury fees he could have avoided had he thought the whole thing through.

RULE NUMBER 36: Deliberately Rework the Things That Have Begun to Work on You

If you determine through your use of the Percentage Rule that something making you angry is taking up too much of your time, you have to implement a game plan to rework your take on what's going on.

Life will happen, and sometimes what happens can be as annoying as hell. And sometimes, no matter what you do, you can't make it go away. This simple fact of life presents you with two options: Remain irritated or rework how you feel about it.

If you choose to rework how you feel, you have to start looking at the problem from a different angle. Find something to get amused about. Or if there's nothing funny about it, infuse it with some metaphysical meaning. It doesn't have to make sense to the rest of the world or be logically defensible. It just has to put whatever it is in a context that fosters calm.

And, of course, if none of this works, refer to Rule Number 30 and Globalize your Pain.

Case in Point: I got all wrapped up in the phone company once. We got in a battle over a phone bill that lasted well over a year. My heart used to pound audibly whenever I had to call them. Anticipating the nonsense and powering down from the argument could mess up my entire morning. At one point it got a little silly, so I sat down and said to myself, "How long are you going to let these people upset your life? Isn't it bad enough that they took your money? Are you really going to let them take your morning too? After all, two things that are clearly more precious than money is my family and my time."

Thus redefined, my anger dissipated and I was able to move on.

Twelve

The How-Dare-You Diaries

This chapter is a devoted to a minor, but persistent, emotional irritant, whose most notable characteristic is its absolute lack of value. An unseemly and small-minded sentiment, it is an equal opportunity annoyance, capable of upsetting the most rational of us, rich or poor, black or white, well-employed or utterly impoverished, educated or otherwise. And while this emotional muckraker has always been around, its modern-day version is a child of ease and entitlement, and, as such, has taken on implications it never has before.

Insult, the topic of this chapter, is the poster boy for putting the way you feel in front of what you need to do. It pulls you off-task, adjusts your agenda, and puts someone you probably don't like in complete charge of your day.

People rode into my courtroom on the backs of insults everyday; some of these insults were deliberate, most were unintended, but others were simply inexplicable. Fights, ongoing neighborhood disputes, small-claims actions that weren't really about money—all of these had angry people coming into my court, spurred on less by the issue at hand but by insult gone unexamined.

Take, for instance, one local professional who took to sending both the prosecutor and the court a barrage of angry communiqués over her grown son's traffic ticket. Incensed by our refusal to allow her to present his case in court for him, she spent more time complaining about issues of respect than she did the problem she sought to solve. Eventually, I had to write her personally, repeating what she had been told all along, which was that if you are not a lawyer you cannot represent other people in court. Days later, I received a thank-you note from her, expressing satisfaction that finally *someone of sufficient status* had bothered to address her concerns. That woman wasted not just a lot of paper and postage in her pursuit of something she didn't need, but also a lot of energy and time.

Consider also a group of people I called my Frequent Flyers. My Frequent Flyers were a cadre of young people who lived their lives from day to day as if tomorrow would never come. Some had high school diplomas; most did not. They slept late, partied hard, had babies. They were also safely ensconced in their parents' middle-class homes, which none of them had any plans to leave. They were sons and daughters of stable parents who, through the sheer force of inertia, were sliding out of middle class. Viewing the occasional visit to court as the cost of doing business, my Frequent Flyers had no intention of letting a little thing like the law interfere with their fun. Thirty days here for driving without a license, ten days there for disorderly conduct—it was all the same to them.

Image is everything to a group of people for whom accomplishments mean little. When cool and style are your only measures of self-worth, someone else's opinion of you speaks to the very essence of your being. So when these young people were insulted, violence was often the result.

"He disrespected me," was the number-one explanation I received in cases of simple assault among the Frequent Flyers. Unfazed by the specter of incarceration, these guys completely lost their composure when someone called them a "punk."

Now, at bottom the Frequent Flyers are really no different from you and me. We all get insulted, and rather regularly. Insult and its aftermath messed up my Thursdays for approximately eight years, and I haven't quite gotten over it yet. Therefore, you ought to take anything said here with a nod to my bias. Be that as it may, I still think I have a valid point.

What happened on Thursdays, you ask? First, let me remind you that as a judge, I have set bond for accused murderers whose victims' families were in court. I've heard testimony from victims in negligent homicide cases, and I have had multiple contacts with ongoing combatants. But I can tell you that my Thursday morning traffic-court sessions were filled with more anger, outrage, and unmitigated arrogance than any other proceeding over which I ever presided.

Traffic court, in fact, allowed me to hone another one of my mother's rules, the one that says you have to re-work your approach to any situation that has begun to work on you (See Rule Number 9—Get Your Mind Right). For almost a year, I was required to warn everyone in the courtroom about their behavior even before the proceedings got started. You could just feel the anticipation and anger buzzing about in the air. You would have thought I was presiding over the O.J. Simpson trial. That's how upset everybody was.

Before I go on, however, I should point out that most people behaved very well in traffic court. And you can't help but applaud your average guy who takes off from work to come to court because he truly believed he was wronged. In fact, I didn't even begrudge those who knew they were wrong but came to court anyway to take a shot at lessening the fine or avoiding points.

The people to whom I refer here are the inexplicable 10 percent who came to traffic court filled with all the righteous indignation of a citizen denied his right to vote. They abused my staff and cried foul when they were asked to follow simple rules. I dealt with people who sent their traffic fines to court with checks smeared in feces. One guy spent $27 in Federal Express fees to send us a $10 fine all in pennies, in an effort to upset us. In fact, the only time I was ever physically threatened in my courtroom was by a guy appearing on a traffic ticket. He jumped out of his chair while in my chambers, leaned right over my desk, and screamed, "I have no respect for you." This tirade was prompted not by the fact that he thought he was innocent—he freely admitted doing 12 miles per hour over the speed limit—but by my refusal to dismiss the ticket on the grounds of some "technicality" he'd heard about on TV.

All of this had me stumped for quite a while. It took me a year or so to figure out just what all of the fuss was about. But I finally came to a couple of useful conclusions. First, it appears, we ordinary citizens take great pride in our law-abiding ways, and it really ticks some of us off when someone suggests we've done something wrong. Consequently, some people saw their traffic ticket as a statement about them, as opposed to a statement as to how fast they were going on Lee Road one Saturday afternoon.

Some suggested to me that their being ticketed in a school zone was the same as saying they did not care about children. Many got on the witness stand and made much of their profession, or the fact that they were a long-time resident. A good one-third got so tied up in the personal hurt that they barely mentioned the infraction at all.

Then there was the cardiovascular surgeon who'd been charged with running a stop sign. He did not contend that the officer was mistaken or that he was responding to an emergency. He simply kept saying that he shouldn't have gotten the ticket. "I told the officer I was a doctor," he said, "The officer was not courteous." He repeated this over and over again. But not once did he mention anything that had a bearing on his case.

Eventually, he became so outdone by the injustice of the whole thing that he broke down crying on the stand. Tears rolled down his face; his lips quivered, and he visibly shook. Forced to stop the proceedings several times when he was periodically rendered unable to speak, I tried everything I could to comfort him. But no amount of rationality or humor did any good. This man simply could not cope with the system's insistence upon treating him like everybody else. It was an affront to his very being.

Second, I determined that people undone by traffic court get into trouble because of how they define the experience. Comfort, like everything else, must obey Rule Number 22, The All-Ramifications Rule. Ease has negative side effects just like anything else. I began to notice that my traffic court defendants were always using terms like "outrage" and "travesty." It seems their lives were so contented that a mere speeding ticket rated as a horrific experience. Worse yet, by the time they got to court they had actually started to feel that way, never thinking that those are the very same words most people reserve to characterize events like September 11.

So, with all these people in mind, ask yourself the following. What happens when you don't get something you feel you deserve? Do life's petty annoyances upset you to no end? Does standing in line or struggling with bureaucratic red tape readjust your mood? Do you dwell on criticism or feel personally wronged when someone forgets your name?

And what do you do when someone doesn't give you the respect to which you feel entitled? Does this dictate what you feel and do long after the insult has come and gone? Here it is in a nutshell: Do you take personally the random nonsense life has in store for us all? And just how much damage do you intend to allow it to do?

So, the next time you're in traffic or something small doesn't go your way ask yourself, "If I had to explain my attitude to a five-year-old, how silly would I feel?"

THE RULES

The Anti-Insult Edicts

RULE NUMBER 37: Know How to Take a Hit

Only you have the power to determine whether someone's opinion of you matters. Therefore, you must give people permission to insult you; otherwise, it won't work.

Do not let the fact that you have a physiological reaction to a comment fool you into believing that there is a real issue there. So, in order to combat that phenomenon, you must remind yourself insults are intended to hurt and upset you. But if you meet them with good-humored disregard, you take all of the fun out of it for the person insulting you. So, if someone insults you, ask yourself:

- Is he right? If so, you have no reason to get angry. Take the information and use it to your advantage. That person may have done you a favor, whether he intended to or not.

- Is he wrong? If so, is it really necessary for you to set the record straight? Make sure you are very clear on this person's relative importance. Does he pay your mortgage, is he your boss, or does he sleep in your bed? If the answer to these or similar questions is "no," then what difference does it make?

In the final analysis, are you going to let people who seek to do you harm determine how you feel?

Case in Point: Someone made a remark to my mom once about my failure to get into Harvard Law School. Instead of reminding this woman how difficult it is to get into that institution, even when you went there as an undergrad, my mother simply responded by agreeing with her. She then went on to complain that I was quite the lazy bohemian in college and that I got exactly what I deserved.

Later, I asked my mother why she agreed so readily with a woman who sought to cause her harm. This is what she said: "She made that remark because she's jealous. She and I both know what her children have done, and none of it is half as impressive as what you and your sister did. That means I've got something she wants, cannot have, and most likely will never get. I have already 'won.'

"If I get angry, it dilutes my victory by satisfying her need to hurt me. But if I let it roll past me, I mess up her whole operation. It's no fun to insult people if they never get upset.

"By the way," she added. "You *were* lazy in college. I told that woman the truth."

RULE NUMBER 38: Avoid Half the Harm

T.S. Eliot said in his play *The Cocktail Party* that half the harm in the world is caused by people who want to feel important.

Recognition, praise, and importance are very seductive things that we're often unprepared for when they come our way. They provide an incredible rush. The problem is, it's hard to see this particular addiction coming because (unlike when you pop a pill or pick up a needle) it's a byproduct of conduct everyone encourages. Once you reap the rewards of success, it starts to feel very good. Unfortunately, that feeling can build on itself in a very negative way. At some point, if you're successful for long enough (or got it through no efforts of your own), you forget what caused everyone to applaud you in the first place and start thinking that you are being praised simply because you're you.

Case in Point: There was an officer in a local police department who lived off the fumes of his position. His arrogance ruled his every waking moment and dictated everything he said. He sparred with attorneys on the witness stand and stuck to his position even when it was eminently clear that he was wrong. There was no contention too outrageous for him to make as long as it supported his original position. Unable to utter "I don't know" or "I don't remember," he would claim knowledge that defied all logic. As a result, more often than not, both juries and I found ourselves not believing a word he said.

▶ *Thirteen*

What's Going on Next Door

One day years ago, when I was a teenager, my mother and I ran into a friend of hers. All was not right at his house. In fact, he was so upset he started telling my mother about the problems he was having with his wife right in front of me. I wasn't yet old enough to know just how little I knew, so when he left I told my mother that I would never put up with the things he did.

In response, my mother shook her head and said the following to me: "You never know what's really going on in somebody else's house unless you live there." Then she paused (that dramatic effect thing again) and said, "How many of your friends have you told about the way we live?"

Realize that *anything* could be going on in the home next door to yours. Reasonable rarely enters into it; rational is seldom the point. Emotions always have a field day in the confines of the home. It's where people feel most free from judgment. It's where they believe they have a right to let go, and since nobody else is looking, it's easier to get away with things.

Compliments of a busy domestic violence docket, I routinely became involved with, if not inundated by, the difficulties next door. Though most of what I saw in court appeared fairly tame compared to my young life on Weyant Avenue, it was still a bit unsettling.

Before I continue, however, I need to explain exactly what kinds of cases I saw. Rarely did I get a situation where blows were thrown or people were actually hurt. Not that these things aren't alarmingly common—it's just that they weren't the bulk of what came before me where I lived. What I saw was mostly everyday drama, along the lines of loud arguments and overturned furniture. In fact, a lot of the people brought in on domestic violence charges were awfully surprised to be there. One bemused husband (along with his unamused wife) declared, "I threw a bowl of ice cream across the room and hit a wall, for heaven's sake. How is that a crime?"

Here's the thing. For years, no one in this country took domestic violence seriously. As a result, many jurisdictions, like mine, eventually adopted "preferred arrest policies." This means that an officer has to explain, in writing, his decision *not* to arrest once he's answered a domestic violence call. And since it's often hard for an officer to tell what's really going on when he shows up at a house and everyone is all excited, odds are that no matter what he sees when he gets there, someone is going to jail. Which means that the next morning they were all on their way to see me. So along with those cases one normally envisions when they hear the phrase "domestic violence," I also saw a lot of behavior that one might not immediately consider violent, and these are the cases that I draw from here. Domestic violence is not a trivial thing, though, so I don't want my concentration on the cases below to leave the impression that it is. They are just the few that I believe can help the average family see where they may be going wrong in a non-criminal sort of way.

You learn a lot about how families operate when you do that kind of volume. You see a lot of the same mistakes made by many different kinds of people, almost all of which implicate a violation of My Mother's Rules. Home is, in fact, the place where my mother's rules are least likely to be obeyed.

Take the Smiths, for example. Mr. Smith was a hard-working 50-year-old with no criminal history. Yet he got hauled into my courtroom for menacing his wife. While he never hit her, Mr. Smith started settling arguments by reminding her that he could — a case of Jackie Gleason humor gone perversely wrong: "One of these days, Alice, POW, straight to the moon."

What Mr. Smith didn't know was that once his wife started to believe his threats, they became a violation of the law. And while her strength and attitude in court were those of a woman not easily

intimidated, I think one day she just got sick of hearing it and decided to call the police.

My probation department's assessment of the family dynamic
found that Mr. Smith wasn't really a bad guy, but had just gotten a little carried away. What had started out as an expedient way
to end an argument became a way of life. He discovered that his
wife would give in when he started that stuff because she didn't
think it was worth the drama. Little by little, though, he'd gotten
louder about it, which prompted her to give in that much faster,
and eventually Mr. Smith wound up nickel-and-diming his wife
into a phone call to the police.

Mr. Smith did not see it coming, though, because he failed to
think about how his actions would appear if others were looking
on. He never would have been doing that kind of thing if other
people could see. He had just gotten into the habit of saying something that brought him immediate relief. People tend to do what
works, and he kept going back to the well. In fact, Mrs. Smith was
more disgusted than scared; she never really thought he'd hit her.
But he had gone too far.

Another common home-bound difficulty I often saw in court
involved Rule Number 20, The Rebound Emotion Rule. This rule
was routinely breached in homes I called High-Volume Households,
where anger becomes such a habit, anyone wanting to be heard
must engage in some kind of dramatic display. Confrontation becomes the status quo. Eventually, the underlying issues lose their
importance because everyone is keeping score. Collecting slights
and storing up hurts: it's all about doing more damage to someone else than they can do to you.

In that kind of atmosphere, the smallest of issues can set off a
full-scale war. Arguments start over anything, because everybody
is always walking around mad. Next thing you know, you have a
whole family in court because dishes were left in the sink.

The Rebound Emotion Rule addresses this problem first by
bringing attention to it. It then suggests that you change how you
define winning and losing. The rule says you lose if you allow someone else to mess up your day by making you mad. It redefines the

argument itself as defeat, and peace and calm as the ultimate victory. This, in turn, should stop the proceedings long enough for the real issues to come to the fore. It will invite an environment that can support rational conversation and that, of course, is the only way to solve a problem.

This is not to say that a mere refusal to engage in combat will in and of itself solve the problems in a High-Volume Household. However, if you keep your eye on the point of the whole thing, as per Rule Number 21, the Turn-Signal Requirement, you'll be better able to distinguish between real problems and the desire to score.

The value of the Turn-Signal Requirement was also driven home in court when I began to see more and more cases of inter-generational domestic violence. Typically, these conflicts arose when some couple's grown children returned home (or, worse yet, when some young, healthy adult never bothered to leave to begin with). Fights would erupt over all manner of things like hours kept and laundry done. Although each problem was seen as an isolated incident, all of these arguments stemmed from a single cause. These families had violated the Turn-Signal Requirement when they failed to redefine their expectations. When Junior returned home, nobody sat down and talked. While they may have discussed a few logistics, they never addressed the important stuff, and expectations were not realigned.

History tells the returning children, "My mother is supposed to take care of me," and of course, their parents feel responsible for them from the moment they are born as a matter of biology. Expectations like that don't simply melt away. They are based on hearty, basic emotions. As a result, both sides continue to feel the same old way even though everything has changed.

Adherence to the Turn-Signal Requirement, however, eliminates that problem. This rule demands announcements. It requires all involved to signal new directions. Change is difficult, especially when one side has no motivation to engage in it. But if you let people know what's about to happen, at least you eliminate the surprise and give the parties involved an opportunity to make an *emotional* adjustment to a different stage in life. Obeying this rule also gives the parties involved an opportunity to discuss the real issues before everyone gets up in arms about some minor thing.

Each of the family doctrine rules I've discussed so far all point in the same direction. They are the small steps one ought to take toward Rule Number 11, Keeping an Eye on the Point of the Whole Thing. Following this rule is like preparing a mission statement for your life that spells out what you're trying to do, then demands that you periodically measure your conduct against that goal.

Abiding by this rule would have been a life saver for Janice Jones. Her legal troubles began when she returned home early from work one day to find her 13-year-old daughter, Marta, naked astride some boy. Suddenly faced with Marta's undulating and ample posterior, Janice found she could not contain herself. So she picked up a broom and took several forceful smacks at Marta's behind, abruptly ending the festivities.

By the time this woman got to court, both the 13-year-old in question and her 14-year-old sister were pregnant. Now, I suppose I could have treated this matter like as a domestic violence case. After all, that was what Janice was charged with, and that was what I was commissioned to resolve. But to me, simply discussing the smack on the behind with a broom when faced with these protruding bellies would have been just silly.

So after we finished with all of the legal stuff, I engaged all three ladies in conversation. "Do you have any idea what was wrong at your house?" I asked Janice. "Do you know what the real problem is here?"

"Nothing is wrong at my house," she replied. "My girls are good kids. They get straight As in school. This was just a misunderstanding."

I tried hard to clear things up for her. Commiserating, confronting, and cajoling, all in turn, I tried everything in my arsenal. But sadly, nothing I said made a difference to her. Janice, unfortunately, had completely lost sight of the point of her job as mother. Neither her ex-con boyfriend nor her own absentee parenting made it onto her radar screen. Janice, instead, had explanations for all of her daughters' difficulties that did not implicate her. Worse yet, when confronted with a problem for which she could not deflect blame, she would contend that no such problem existed.

Unable to clarify the underlying absence of logic that defined her situation, I decided to leave theory alone and instead focus on some practical applications. "Have you helped them get support orders from the children's fathers? Sixteen or not, the boys have to step up to the plate."

She responded with an air of businesslike authority. "We're trying to find out the boys' last names now. And as soon as we do, I'm going to have them both in court."

Of course, most people do not have the kinds of concerns that Janice had. But then again, I bet a lot of us have problems at home that we can't even identify, not to mention fix. The doctrine of family will, however, help you figure out what's wrong. It will shed light into the darkest home and help you handle the worst of habits.

Let's take this inquiry home, the place where you're most likely to get stuck on stupid because the rest of the world isn't looking at you. People get used to things very quickly, and we rarely revisit cause and effect once our actions become habits. This presents a special problem at home, since in the absence of outside observers we are even less likely to reconsider what we do.

With this understanding in mind, ask yourself if you have fallen into a pattern of behavior like the Smiths. Has something odd taken on the look of ordinary because you've been at it for so long? Has the dynamic between you and your partner taken on a life of its own, one that neither one of you intended and now seem unable to control?

Do you live in a High-Volume Household? Does your family operate one level below irate on a daily basis? How many times have you and your significant other had the same argument in different forms? And do you really think there is something magical about the fifty-seventh time you say the very same thing that will make it easier to understand?

THE RULES

The Doctrine of Family III

Like I said, you have to do your best work at home, which is why the Doctrine of Family has so many rules.

RULE NUMBER 39: The Peanut Gallery Rule

This rule asks you to imagine that you have an audience at home. It reminds us that we often misbehave simply because no one's watching what we do. So every once in a while, you should ask yourself the following questions: Would you still be doing what you're doing if other folks could see? Would you feel comfortable divulging the evening's activities to a judge?

If the answer to either of these question is "no," then you must ask yourself why. Is it merely a matter or privacy or is something ridiculous going on?

RULE NUMBER 40: Watch for the Nickel-and-Dime Effect

The Nickel-and-Dime Effect gets rolling because the behaviors that bring it into play don't have immediate consequences. It's the danger in the distance between what you want now and what can go wrong one day. You start nickel-and-diming when you assume you'll have more strength tomorrow than you have today. Nickel-and-diming ignores the cumulative effect of enjoyable wrongs that pave the way to an addiction.

In order to keep this kind of small-step logic at bay, you have to make conscious decisions about the things you will not do. This list should include small destructive habits that are of specific concern to you. You have to know what kind of people you need not be around, the kind who pull you off track and make you forget what it is you've got to do. Problem foods, intoxicants of all varieties, and out-of-bounds objects of your sexual desire ought to make this list as well. Included, too, should be those odds and ends that, as a rule, don't bother the general public, but have a way of messing with you.

It also helps if you have a few cheats to signal an emerging nickel-and-dime concern. For instance, watch for key nickel-and-dime expressions like, "Just this once," or more dangerous yet, "One more time won't matter." Never allow yourself to say either one of those things without naming out loud the monster you'll eventually run into if things go too far. And under no circumstances should your ever utter any nickel-and-dime expression more than once about any one particular thing.

Case in Point: My mother and I are both streak eaters. We'll find some new food we like and that's all we'll eat for a month. I lost my mind over Swell Bubble Gum once, killing a bag of fifty in 24 hours and showing up at Walgreens the very next day so I could do it all again. I kept this up for a month or so until it almost became an everyday event.

Although that particular time my appetites got the best of me, it doesn't happen often, because my mother and I have two methods for dealing with this particular propensity. We'll refuse to even try something that we think we might really like. We'll say out loud, "I can't have any because I might not be able to stop." The other thing we do is make sure we buy only a limited quantity. Finally, we draw a line at the third trip. Specific, arbitrary lines in the sand are essential to abating the nickel-and-dime effect.

Fourteen

Reconciliation

I had a young lady in my courtroom once who I'll call Sally Tyler. She was brought in on a domestic violence charge for pouncing on her mom. Sally was 25 or so. She had long blond hair, three small children, and no high school diploma. Her mother, Donna, was relatively young herself, even if she didn't look it. At 43, I could have sworn she had the words "I'm tired" etched in wrinkles on her face.

This is a story about one's failures coming home to live with you. By all accounts, including Donna's, she was not a very good mom. Small-scale drug use and a string of less-than-appropriate men tended to fill up Donna's days. Predictably, Sally fell victim to her mother's minimalist maternal efforts and went on to fail in all the ways children raised that way are prone to fail. Sally had left her mother's house at 18, full of the particularly ignorant kind of arrogance that comes with youth. Leading a life dedicated to the Rationale of the Right Now, in a few short years Sally had no option but to return to the one place she swore she'd never set foot in again.

The fight that brought the Tylers to court happened some six months after Sally returned home and decided that she didn't like *her* mother's rules. Though neither woman could recall exactly what the fight was about, it was quite an altercation, involving both thrown furniture and broken glass.

Sally pled guilty to domestic violence, and after taking care of all of the procedural stuff, I asked her if she had anything she wanted to say. Needing no further encouragement, Sally embarked on a pain-filled rant that started with the outrage of the moment and ended with a free-fall account of all of her mother's mistakes.

Now normally, this is not something a judge wants to get involved in. We do volume in a municipal court and really don't have the time for that kind of thing. But these ladies were still doing a slow boil, and they had to go home together. So I thought it would be best if I addressed some of their concerns while there was an armed officer in the room.

Soon after our conversation began, it became clear what both women wanted. Sally was looking to get off the hook. She wanted the world to know that none of it was her fault, not even her failure to get a high-school diploma or the three children she couldn't support. Sally, in fact, didn't really believe she was responsible for the knot she put on her mother's head. But for her mother's failures, her reasoning went, none of this would have occurred. Donna, on the other hand, was trying to make things right, not only for her daughter's sake, but to soothe her own guilt as well. Her remedial maternal efforts took the form of a place to stay and a whole lot of advice. The former Sally believed she was owed, the latter she did not want. As one might imagine, she was thankful for neither, and she made sure her mother knew it.

All of this emotional foolishness left Sally and Donna quite out of control. Having flown on the fumes of anger so long, they had forgotten how to land. Each one focused solely on the fact that she had a defensible point of view. Both women had stopped listening to one another and could find no common ground.

Once I realized what kind of trouble they were in, I referred them to the appropriate rules. Explaining the frustration inherent in focusing solely on things you cannot get, I told Sally she needed to accept the fact that the stable-childhood ship had sailed. "While torturing your mother will make you feel better momentarily," I said, "in the long run, it will not get you what you want. When faced with something unfortunate that you cannot change, you are left with two options: continue to pursue that which was unavailable to you, or redefine your wants and redirect your efforts, and start chasing satisfaction."

I also suggested that despite the way it might feel at first, moving on isn't the same thing as letting her mother off the hook. Nor did it imply that she didn't have the right to feel the way she did. It just meant that she was choosing not to continue to be hurt by things no one could change.

That's when I brought in my own personal theory on paying for sin on the back end. The interest is a bitch. As a result, I told Donna she needed to get over feeling abused because her belated efforts to do the right thing were not met with applause and thank-yous. She bought and paid for what she was getting, and she needed to look at it that way. "If you look at it like that," I said, "you won't feel so unappreciated and her attitude will be easier to deal with. You have to be willing to suck a bit of this up in order to help put right what you did wrong."

Then we talked about rebound emotions and how to stop them from ricocheting around the house. I explained that it wasn't an either/or situation, that they both had a job to do. I followed up with more specific, practical advice, but I think you get the point. All that was left for them to decide whether they were going to make the situation they had work.

"This is where we are," I told the ladies, "and the question is simply this: do you want to continue to battle one another, or do you want to start feeling better?"

■■■

I told you Donna and Sally's story because it represents, in the extreme, the problems so many of us face when it comes to dealing with how we feel, especially when we are trying to feel our way beyond a past that may not have served us well. I am trying to tell you the very same thing I told them, which is that when you are faced with something unpleasant, you can decide how it will affect you by redefining what it means. You can, in short, decide to reconcile *what is* with *what you need right now.* Reconciliation is not about forgiveness, although that is often its byproduct. Nor is it an exercise in simply learning to suck it up. It is a process of understanding.

It is a purposeful attempt to excise emotion and view the facts that make up your history, as a researcher would. Then, once you better understand your past, reconciliation requires you to deal with what happened in a way that will do you some good.

The Rules of Reconciliation also work with ongoing difficulties. They will help you feel your way past ordinary irritations or above difficult circumstances. Typically, people *know* what they should do but aren't able to *feel* in a way that allows them to do it. Following the Rules of Reconciliation, however, will permit you to do just that. They will allow you to pick the proper emotion for whatever occasion you come across.

Unfortunately, reconciliation is not always an easy sell, because it flies in the face of two fervent American demands. We are fanatics for both fairness and feeling better, and we typically want both right away. We want the books to balance, and we want to hold the scale. Ours is a courtroom culture, one that tells us to take sides and demand compensation for anything that makes us unhappy. People in societies as fortunate as ours have a hard time with reconciliation.

I know that it is a difficult process. For years, I did not like my father; for a minute there, I was also mad at Mom. They were both adults, I reasoned, and as such they both did exactly what they wanted and meant everything they did. I had no way of knowing that it was an unquiet mind, as opposed to an unfeeling nature, that made my father chase my mother down the street. Nor was I aware of the bigger picture my mother saw each time she made the decision to stay.

Yes, growing up with Daddy did me a bit of harm, but the simple fact is this. Nobody ever asked him whether he wanted to be a little nuts. And I am quite sure he never bowed his head and asked God to make him crazy so he could torment his wife and kids.

Understanding these facts takes intent out of the equation and replaces it with dumb luck, the very same animal that has killed millions of people over the centuries with your basic floods, your random hurricane, your typical earthquakes, and the odd famine or two. I see the big picture, and I know there is no reason why great tragedy should exempt me. So, as unpleasantness goes, I think I got off light, and I am willing to live with that.

Besides, if I had continued to assign blame, I would have missed the best parts of my father. Psychosis, mania, mental illness notwithstanding, Daddy did right by us.

Remember the mean-streets urban poverty into which my mother was born? Well, my father started out life in the West Virginia, outhouse, not-enough-to-eat kind of poverty. All of five feet, two inches tall, a black man born abjectly poor in 1919, he was not supposed to make it. With an angry, invalid father who, family legend has it, Daddy tried to strangle once, Bill Toler became his family's sole source of income when he was just thirteen.

My sister and I, however, were born into middle-class comfort. The very same personal peccadilloes that made Daddy break windows also made him a financial success. He worked seven days a week, and took one two-week vacation in all of the 36 years I knew him. Daddy made a lot of money and he gave it all to us. He happily paid for four separate degrees for my sister and me, three of which came with Ivy League price tags. Unable to utter the word "no" in our presence, he always gave us everything we wanted. My father's value did not, however, end with what he did for us financially. Daddy was wicked brilliant, a man who, when not enveloped by his psychosis, could think rings around most people. He had a tremendous sense of humor and, as soon as he possibly could, he treated my sister and me like adults. He fed me a sense of irreverence about the status quo that I still enjoy today.

When I'd come home from college we used to sit in the courtyard sipping scotch and laughing about all kinds of stuff. There was no subject matter (other than his personal history) that was off limits for him. We talked about sex and work and men and law and white and black and right and wrong. I could tell him anything. He told me once, "You know I'd let you and that guy have sex in the house 'cause I know you all are doing it at school." Then he laughed and said, "But you know how your mother is."

I recognize, too, that living with Daddy allowed me to reap at least some of the benefits of the rougher road. Things that bother

other people intensely barely rate for me. Despite my experiences with racial discrimination, I do not carry the emotional baggage that often comes along with it. Having very little emotional money left at the end of any given month, I never bought the sense of shame and denigration they tried to sell me in elementary school. Nor do I feel victimized by the extra challenges that come with being black.

Moreover, in determining the value of what happened to me, I also take into account those things that didn't happen as well. In the absence of all that household drama, who knows what kind of adolescent errors I might have made? Since this isn't a movie of the week, I will not suggest that everything is fine. My Mother's Rules have helped me live a better life, but they can neither change who I am nor what it was I saw. There are still days when I see the smallest of problems as a promise of catastrophe. On other days, I simply do not sleep. I worry still about things that, for the most part, have no consequence, and I cannot tell you what it is, but some days I don't feel safe. These things I believe are also gifts from Daddy, partly by virtue of living conditions, and partly through our genes.

I am who I am, and that means that I will always have to deal with my inherently fearful nature. I know too that I will continue to do battle with the emotional memories of Weyant Avenue. An uproarious youth is one of those gifts that keeps on giving. And while I would like to hear life in much more sedate tones, as opposed to the whispers and screams that define me, I wouldn't trade my childhood for any other, no matter how serene. In the end, psychosis notwithstanding, the good in my father far outweighed the bad, and I consider whatever shudders that remain from my rattled youth as collateral damage—friendly fire, so to speak, unintended injuries and all.

We were not, I contend, a dysfunctional family; challenged, yes, I'll admit to that, but we operated well. In fact, we did far better than just get by. We thrived, we loved, and nobody walked away mad.

I feel good about both then and now, which is, in the end, all you can really ask for. I am reconciled but not resigned. I am at peace with what I have while still purposefully pursuing what I want. Composed, I guess is what you'd call it.

Why? Because I get the joke.

It is funny, you know, if you look at it right. All that nonsense we humans tend to get into often defies all logic. The thing is, you have got to know when to get excited and when to shrug things off.

And then there is the joy thing, the part of the puzzle my sister always knew how to find. If you get with the program and cultivate some measure of ease, you will be in a better position to feel the joy that we so often overlook. Things will get truly ugly soon enough, for all of us. Whether illness, financial disaster, or unexpected death, we will all suffer at some point in our lives. The Rule of Inclusion never gets repealed, and you have to learn to live with that. But if you have not wasted your time getting upset over nonsense, you will be in a better frame of mind to tackle the tough stuff when it comes.

Of course, there are those circumstances that are so extreme that no amount of emotional insight can conquer them completely. But even in the context of terrible things, there are still emotional choices to be made. Half the battle is in believing that you can overcome them. The other half is in knowing what you're dealing with and how to work through it.

Of course, my story is only half-told at this point. There is so much left for me to do. I am 47 as of this writing, technically middle aged. Menopause has already fired its first warning shot across my bow. God willing, I have another 40 or 50 years to go, and in that time the Beast will have ample opportunity to raise her ugly head again. While I have a handle on my lesser self, I know I will never defeat it. Even now, no matter what I do, some days I am still the little girl on Weyant Avenue who, no matter how hard she tries, cannot control the world enough to keep her calm. I continue to engage in perpetual movement in an effort to keep sane. The devil of my idle mind still knows nothing but disaster.

The thing is, I've learned to be content with a certain level of discontent. Some days I even find it funny. I truly believe that God does love a good joke. And considering the hellishness going on in a whole lot of this world, I feel no need to complain.

So take whatever you can from these rules and approach your emotional self with a sense of bravado and control. See what you can do about feeling better all of the time. My mother once described herself to me as accepting, not of those things she could control but of those that she could not. Accepting that life is the way it is allowed her to control how she felt, and once she did that she was better able to control everything else.

THE RULES

The Rules of Reconciliation

RULE NUMBER 41: Show Some Passion for the Proper Things

It is very easy to become consumed by everyday emotional adventures. Traffic, bosses, schedules, waiting; it can be so constant and so immediate that it sucks up all of your attention. If, however, you allow the mundane to become your focus, sooner or later the small stuff will become the sum total of your life.

There are a whole lot of different ways you can live any particular moment. Each one, in and of itself, is both an option and opportunity. You can fill it with worries, despair, or regret. You can spend it nursing old hurts and anger. Or you can put it to work for you. You can be productive in it—take a swing in some fight you *need* to fight, and see how far you get. You can fill it with calm or an act of love or with a simple pleasant memory. Libraries, community, worship, and conversation are all free. And there is a biological basis for the calm we feel when we engage in these kinds of things.

The context and meaning of your life is established from moment to moment. So never forget to feed your soul even when feeding the body is a difficult thing to do.

Case in Point: My mother says books saved her life. They gave her somewhere to go other than the unpleasant places she lived. She thinks that's why she avoided some of the mistakes others made.

"You have to believe in something beyond what you see," Mom told me once when I was trying to fall apart.

RULE NUMBER 42: The Kathy Code: Wrap Your Arms Around It All

My sister, Kathy, was born with the innate ability to enjoy things. Armed with the capacity to find the fun in just about any situation, my sister can see what's wonderful in just about every aspect of the world. She can have as much fun with the lowliest thug as she can with the rich and refined. My sister has the most incredible ability to throw her head back and laugh.

It took me 30 years to figure out what my sister *always* knew. Kathy was always enjoying herself because she was able to wrap her arms around the depth and breadth of the variety in this world. She looked for what she could find entertaining when she met up with new and different. My sister purposely courted joy, and she always understood its intrinsic value.

We lived in the same home, with the same father, and saw all of the same stuff, but she never took it with her when she left that house. Kathy had other things on her mind.

Now I have learned how to manufacture joy if you put enough effort into it. There is something to relish in almost everything, if you take the time to find it. The problem is, we often see this kind of pleasure-searching as flighty and unnecessary, something that does not serve a real purpose in a rational world. But since our moods and feelings unwittingly dictate so much of what do, wouldn't it behoove us to cultivate the most positive attitude we can?

Case in Point: The stock market does better on sunny days than it does when it's overcast. The same economic factors apply, whether it's cloudy or bright, but apparently, our perception of them is altered by the mood we're in. Emotions moving money, trumping numbers and common sense. Can you imagine that?

RULE NUMBER 43: The Dumb-Luck Rule

Sometimes things do not make sense, and no matter how hard you try, all the dots will not connect. In life, there is no final scene where everyone's true motives and allegiances are divulged. There will be no point (while we're still breathing, at least) at which everything that seems random will all start making sense.

This rule says that you can't get all caught up in that if you want to stay productive. Coincidences happen, dumb luck is real, and both can explain a whole lot of what goes on. Get comfortable with that and you'll feel a lot better, no matter what goes wrong.

▶ *Fifteen*

Afterword

It took me six years to write this book and, as you might imagine, in that time a number of things have changed. Most notably, I am no longer unemployed. As I write this I am in the midst of my first season as the judge on the nationally syndicated television show *Divorce Court. Divorce Court* is a fun show, voyeuristic to be sure, but not devoid of value if you look at it in the right way. Those who care to watch the show will see me search for the humor in daily drama, render a decision based on the law, and hopefully share a bit of wisdom.

Other things have changed as well. My children are older, as am I. Menopause's warning shot has turned into a full-fledged conflagration. Be that as it may, I have learned a great deal about patience in the last few years. Between kid-pitch baseball, five-hour track meets and a variety of music and martial arts lessons, I have learned to wait with greater ease, just like so many other mothers. This new ability could not have come at a better time, as my job now requires a weekly commute between Cleveland and LA. There is nothing like a five-hour flight twice a week to test an impatient woman's resolve.

Some things remain the same, though. I am still married, as anyone who watches *Divorce Court* knows. Believing as I do that there is no greater teacher than experience, I often refer to the work in progress that is my marriage on the show. I also remain a control freak, a woman who engages in daily battle with terms like "what if" and "maybe," which leads me to my latest and momentarily greatest concern.

I had reservations about writing this book. In it, I have put the least of me on paper for the world to see. I have aired my family's dirty laundry and tried to make comprehensible to readers things that I barely understand myself. Having done so, I face the very real possibility that people will think less of me and all of the people I love.

But I truly believe it is worth the risk. I am firmly convinced that I learned something of great value both on Weyant Avenue and on the bench, something that should be shared. In a time where experts abound and syndromes proliferate, I feel we all could use a dose of good old-fashioned common sense. In a country where we seem to ride the fumes of insult everywhere we go, and all manner of emotional outbursts erupt at the slightest provocation, it's time for us to revisit our emotional lives with an eye toward greater *self*-regulation.

To that end, I have risked the misunderstandings and negative responses that may accompany *My Mother's Rules* and hereby offer you a lifetime of costly lessons learned, for the price of $15.

APPENDIX

My Mother's Rules: A Handy Digest

The Underlying Principles

1: The Smith and Wesson Test

Most people say that they can't help the way they feel. This is neither good nor true. This is especially true when we talk about changing how we feel. In order to be a good emotional manager, you must decide that you have the ability to choose how you want to feel, and the best way to do that is to take The Smith and Wesson Test. Ask yourself, "If someone put a gun to my head, would I be able to stop screaming at my kids?" If the answer to that question is "yes," then your problem is not so much about ability as it is a matter of motivation.

2: Work Your Emotions Like a Job

Practice. You have to address how you feel through what you do and the way you look at things. You must decide that you will *make* your emotions follow your actions and not the other way around. Don't wait to change unproductive behavior until you *feel* like doing something else—you have to do the right thing when it feels all wrong. Keep doing it no matter what. Then slowly but surely what you feel will start to follow what you do.

The Codification of Attitude and Outlook

3: The Bathroom Mirror Mandate

In order to comply with this rule, you must think through all of your major mistakes. Search out their causes, peruse them for patterns, and then figure out what they say about you. Reexamine the things other people say to you, not in order to determine whether they are right, but in an effort to understand how they came to their conclusion. Even if you are not who they say you are, you have to consider this: is what you're doing conveying something other than what you intend? The point of all of this soul-searching is for you to gain a heightened state of awareness. Remember, your faults and weaknesses will never hurt anyone else as much as they'll hurt you. But if you know what they are and understand how they work, they will be much less likely to do you harm.

4: The Rule of Inclusion

Most of us are not born on the south side of Chicago. Lots of us got better; some of us got worse. Be that as it may, we all have stuff to deal with. Big, small, or otherwise, everyone has some kind of misfortune. This rule requires us to acknowledge, out loud, that there is nothing so special about any one of us that exempts us from misfortune. My mother's answer to the question "Why me?" is always "Why *not* you? Why should you get a free pass on all of that the pain and suffering the whole world has known since the beginning of time?" Distress is all a part of it. No one has singled you out. And if you can ban the feeling of being unfairly targeted that often accompanies misfortune, you can remove an entire layer of emotional baggage that you really don't need.

5: No Matter What, Keep Coming

Absent willpower, all of the opportunity in the world doesn't mean a thing. In order to keep coming, you must decide that neither your situation nor the people around you can define who you are or determine what you can do. I'm not saying that you can do anything if you try. Sometimes, no matter what you do, there will be some things you can't overcome. But even if effort will not guarantee success, this rule requires you to acknowledge that its absence guarantees failure.

6: Get Amused

There are very few things in life that are not just a little bit funny. If you learn to get some pleasure out of your failings, the whole world will be easier to take. One's sense of humor is invaluable when things aren't going well. It makes tolerable those terrible things you can neither change nor avoid. Getting amused is much more useful than getting frustrated, angry, or mad. The problem is you have to work on the first one, while the last three come naturally.

The Rules Related to Cool

7: Identify the Dog That's Barking

Don't just feel something and keep moving. Stop and give it a name. You cannot be in control of something if you don't know what it is. So at any given time, on any given day, you should be willing to, *and in fact make a habit of,* asking yourself the following question: *What am I feeling and why?* By naming the source of your dismay, you can better isolate it. It will help you realize that it was the kids and the traffic that made you angry, and not what your boss just said. That way you're less likely to cuss out the wrong person in the wrong situation, and add to the troubles you already have.

8: Then Meet Fido at the Door

A shifting mood always announces itself. You just have to learn to listen. If you're really in touch with your feelings, you can hear them howling long before they reach your door.

After a while you'll start noticing shifts in mood without making the effort to do so. You'll see Fido walking up the drive and know just how big he is.

9: Get Your Mind Right

This simply means that once you realize that you are sporting an emotion that is not doing you any good, you must decide to feel differently. The trick is to pick a *specific* emotion that you believe will serve you better and consciously decide to adopt it.

10: Learn to Act in Opposition to How You Feel

In order to do this, follow the steps below.

A. Give It Voice

When I say give it voice, I mean exactly that. Don't just think it. Actually open up your mouth and make some noise. Or better yet, put it down on paper. When you say something out loud, or see it in writing, it helps put shape to an unformed idea, and once anything takes on concrete form, it's easier to handle.

B. Always Have a Game Plan

Whenever you are scheduled to encounter one of your triggers, form a game plan to help you through it. There are lots of ways to do this and you can think up some on your own. But the following four are the ones I use. They may give you some ideas.

1. *Walk around it.* The easiest way to stay out of trouble is to stay away from where it lives. While I recognize that I have the right to go just about anywhere, I also acknowledge that there are certain places a person like me ought not be.

2. *Fight it out.* Of course, you can't always avoid things. Sometimes you simply have to stand your ground and fight. But in doing so, you must remember that the first battle you must engage in is always with yourself. You have to give voice to any weakness that might be implicated in what you are about to face.

3. *Enlist assistance.* Find somebody in your life who loves you and is not afraid to give you a little crap. Tell them what it is you need to do and ask them to help you do it. You can't get mad at somebody for doing what you

asked them to do, even if in the process of doing it, they manage to get on your nerves.

4. *Take it to another level.* When faced with something you don't want to do, pretend that it is something other than what it is. It does not have to be reasonable, nor does it need to make sense to any one but you. It is simply a means to an end, a way to get you where you're going.

The Doctrine of Family

11: Keep Your Eye on the Point of the Whole Thing

Every once in a while you have to step away from what you're doing and make sure you are still heading in the direction you originally intended to go. Dealing with everyday problems and immediate feelings can obscure your ultimate goal. If you don't keep your eye on the point of the whole thing, sometimes you wander off the path.

12: Draw a Clear Line

There are some compromises that should never be made and some behaviors that should never be tolerated. This rule requires us to define these things clearly and to stand by those decisions we make. Being cool and calm is one thing; being taken advantage of is quite another. Be specific. Concrete things are much easier to understand and thus much easier to defend.

The Principles of Parenting

13: Make Sure You're Seeing What You've Got

Our natural tendency is to defend our children against all comers, including legitimate criticism. But you can't help your children overcome their weaknesses if you don't know what they are. So, you must consciously fight the urge to make excuses for them.

14: The Rule of the Rougher Road

To construct a childhood for your kids without want or disappointment is misleading. In order to be on your children's team, sometimes you can't be on their side. In the end, you have to prepare your children to live in a world that doesn't love them as you do. If you live cool, your kids will be cool, and there is nothing better than that.

15: It Isn't So Much What You Say

It's easier for people, including your kids, to process criticism when there is nothing at stake. Regaling them with their weaknesses isn't productive when they've just done something wrong, because a whole lot of unproductive emotions get in between them and what you want them to hear. Being defensive, frightened, or otherwise upset doesn't help anyone's listening skills. Instead, share this essential negative information with them when everything is going well.

16: Introduce Them To The Emotional World

Children need to know how to handle more than just their own emotional stuff. They also need to understand the emotional implications of living in the world. They need to know that other people feel and think in ways that might be very different from their own. The key to this particular rule is giving them the information far before they need it, and in a way that does not resemble "telling them what to do." When you do this, you want to be seen as sharing secrets and not restricting their behavior.

The Continuing Education Requirements

17: Beware the Comfort of Deciding It's Not Your Fault: The Rule Against Teching

There are usually several factors that contribute to any problem. As a result, you can almost always find someone or something, other than yourself, to blame for the ones you have—"technically." This can lead to "Teching." Teching occurs when you search through a mess that *you* made for one small thing that somebody else did wrong. You don't get to do that. Ever. If you blame others, you might get some sympathy. If you accept responsibility, you gain control.

18: Do Not Believe the Lies You Tell Other People

People tend to make a lot of excuses for what they do. No one likes to feel stupid, and it is no fun to admit that you are wrong. Though excuses make you feel better, that sense of relief comes at the cost of control. And if you lose too much of that, you go into victim mode. If you need to move the truth around a little in order not to feel like a fool in front of others, well, go right ahead. If, however, you do choose to massage the facts, you must still make a clear, concerted, and conscientious effort to remember and believe the truth. A lie can actually start feeling like the truth if you tell it often enough. And if you don't pay attention, the day may come when you can no longer tell the difference between the two.

The Doctrine of Family II

19: Understand the He, Me, and We of It

There are three people in any marriage. You, your spouse, and the thing you become when the two of you get together. When you get married, you *must* change. Things that worked well when you were single will not necessarily work any more. You have to see how the best and worst in you brings out the best or worst in the other person. Then you must adjust what you do so that things work out the way you want and need them to, for the both of you.

20: The Rebound Emotion Rule

Rebound emotions are emotional background noise that keep you from hearing what was said, so you can stick instead with what you think. They emerge when people get used to feeling a certain way about other people, especially the ones they live with. And after a while, no matter what the other person does, it will be interpreted in a way that fulfills old expectations. A decision has to be made when rebound emotions are ricocheting around a house. This must be done when no one is angry: you must simply start a conversation about the entire scope of things. And when you do, start with the positive and talk about how you'd like things to be. Then tell everybody that with a little work, you think it can really be that way. Then *you* make the first compromise before you ask for one in return.

21: The Turn-Signal Requirement

People are a lot less likely to run into you if they know where you're going. You put your turn signal on while driving, and you should use it at home as well. You get what you ask for. People know what you tell them. They will understand what you explain. Just because somebody loves you doesn't mean he or she can read your mind. Your family cannot do right by you unless they know what that entails. Never underestimate the value of having a rational conversation, one that occurs right after sex, a satisfying meal, or an unexpected compliment. This should be a conversation that expresses what you want in a nonthreatening, but serious, manner and you should have this conversation *before* you do whatever it is that your partner may not be expecting.

The Act of Balancing

22: The All-Ramifications Rule

Nothing is ever all good or all bad. Good things carried too far can become a problem. Likewise, bad stuff, if responded to appropriately, can strengthen and teach you better than all of the instruction in the world. With this in mind, keep a cautious eye on the good things in your life to make sure they stay good, while making a conscious effort to find constructive to make use of the bad things.

23: Know When to Holler for Help

Just as the All-Ramifications Rule requires that you should never label anything as all good or all bad, so it is with experts. You have to understand what they are for and not believe everything they say. Their words, thoughts, and advice must be examined just like anything else. They are human too, despite the many letters strung behind their names; they have odd points of view, predilections, and biases just like anyone else. But if used correctly and with constant vigilance, they can really help you out.

The Rules of Persuasion

24: Understand Your Audience

Often your ability to persuade has little to do with the rationality of your argument. Emotions, more than logic, dictate what people both hear and believe. So you have to understand what your audience is feeling before you can get your audience to understand you. To do this you must first understand what it is *you* are feeling— and then set those feelings aside. You can't hear what someone is saying if you are busy, say, defending yourself, being insulted, or just standing there disgusted. So step back and pretend you are eavesdropping on two other peoples' conversation. Listen simply to understand.

25: Wait Until They're Ready

When it comes to persuasion, timing is a very important factor that people tend to overlook. Anger does little to clear your head, increase your vocabulary, or enhance your ability to speak. If you discuss something important while the other parties involved are angry, you will not be able to get your point across. The yeller can't express himself well, and the yellee is too busy defending himself to be able to absorb and understand.

Sometimes, all it takes to win an argument is to bring the issue up at a time when the wrong emotions won't get in the way. If your husband, say, is currently feeling good about you, he is more likely to feel good about what you have to say.

26: Start Where Other People Are and Slowly Walk Them Home

You can't get people to change their minds by telling them that they're wrong. Moreover, people simply hate to change, and they don't much like to admit that they're wrong, either. A successful emotional approach to persuasion must take all of this into account. When arguing, most people focus on the weaknesses in the other guy's position to the exclusion of all else. However, if you do that, the other guy will think you don't understand what he's saying and he'll keep repeating what he's already said. Remember, there is some level of logic that rests somewhere in most of what anybody says. It may not be good logic, but it still makes sense to the person who says it. In order to be persuasive, you must be able to address your opponent's entire understanding of a situation. Then you must repeat it to him, so he knows you see his point. Once you've got him listening with less emotional static in the way, start walking him home slowly.

The Commandments of Culture

27: Beware Entitlement Inflation

People who feel entitled to everything get disappointed a lot. The problem is that sometimes it is hard to tell the difference between what you are actually owed and what you simply want. In order to avoid confusing the two, you must keep a limited, clearly defined, and specific list of entitlements in your head. That way, the next time you feel abused or misused, you can return to that list and see if the thing you've been denied is on it. If not, it might be best to just get over it.

28: Increase Your Nonsense Threshold

Judging things and finding fault is basic to human nature. Unfortunately, such judgments can keep you from enjoying new and different things that really can't do you any harm. They also add to your worry quotient new items that really shouldn't rate, making your life seem more precarious and beleaguered than it really is. Remember, small things only bother small people. So relax. Get over it. And realize that sometimes you have to *work* to make it not matter.

29: Watch Your Superlatives

Examine your working vocabulary for evidence of the extreme. Plow through all your daily commentary for unnecessary value judgments and negative assumptions. If you call all misfortune "horrific" and every upset "traumatic," your base emotionality will go up and your tolerance level will go down. Next thing you know, you will be getting upset over smaller and smaller things.

30: Globalize Your Pain Quotient

Let's say you do not live in Afghanistan, or in the drought-ravaged Sudan. But the lady in front of you has 30 coupons, a personal check (but no check-cashing card), and at least one question about the price of every product in her cart. What is there *really* to be upset about in that situation?

The Anger Avoidance Amendments
31: The First-Wave Rule

The next time you start to feel afraid or angry, when no immediate physical threat presents, you must condition yourself to do *nothing* for a least a second or two. Make a point of isolating and feeling each part of your anger's physical aspects. Note the rapid heartbeat, the warming face, and the sudden desire to act. Stop and purposefully experience each and every part of if it. While you're doing that, think about how interesting the whole process is in an objective and detached way. This inventory, as silly as it sounds, serves two purposes. First, it will help you recognize the storm the next time it comes around. The second purpose is simply buying time. There is nothing quite as important as placing a moment of rationality between what you *feel* and what you *do*.

32: Beware the Rationale of the Right Now

Accept that discomfort is a part of life. If you do not expect to feel good all of the time, it will be easier for you to focus beyond your frustration and address the problem at hand. So get comfortable with your discomfort. Accept that on occasion you'll be displeased, annoyed, unhappy, or otherwise upset. That way you can avoid responding emotionally to a logistical concern.

33: Don't Let Your Emotions Straddle Events

Whenever something gets you worked up, make sure you talk yourself down from that agitated state before you move on to something else. Give voice to each upsetting occurrence as it happens. Then tell yourself, out loud, that you won't let it bleed into the rest of your life. Intersperse elevating events among your tragedies. The worse things get, the more important it is to show a passion for the proper things.

34: Make Sure You Know Where the Mad's Supposed to Go

Since your body has no way of knowing why it's all worked up, angry often ends up going places it has no business being. Typically, misplaced anger falls on the first available target, or the easiest kill. While your body wants to feel better, it doesn't want to get hurt.

So before acting on the source of any anger, you must consider all people whose only fault is weakness or proximity. Understand that this is what tends to happen and keep an eye out for it.

35: The Percentage Rule

In order to remain in compliance with this rule, all you have to do is step back on occasion and do a priority check. List the things you're doing and how much time they're taking up. Then ask yourself: What was the point of the whole thing when you started out? And did that somehow get lost in the process of getting the thing done?

36: Deliberately Rework the Things That Have Begun to Work on You

Life will happen, and sometimes what happens can be as annoying as hell. And sometimes no matter what you do you can't make it go away. This simple fact of life presents you with two options: remain irritated or rework how you feel about it. If you choose to rework how you feel, you have to start looking at the problem from a different angle. Find something to get amused about. Or if there's nothing funny about it, infuse it with some metaphysical meaning. It doesn't have to make sense to the rest of the world or be logically defensible. It just has to put whatever it is in a context that fosters calm.

The Anti-Insult Edicts

37: Know How to Take a Hit

Only you have the power to determine whether someone's opinion of you matters. Therefore, you must give people permission to insult you; otherwise, it won't work. Do not let the fact that you have a physiological reaction to a comment fool you into believing that there is a real issue there. So, in order to combat that phenomenon, you should ask yourself the following whenever someone throws an insult your way: What is he trying to achieve, and are you going to let him do it? Insults are intended to hurt and upset you. But if you meet them with good-humored disregard, you take all of the fun out of it for the person who is insulting you. In the final analysis, are you going to let people who seek to do you harm determine how you feel?

38: Avoid Half the Harm

Recognition, praise, and importance are very seductive things that we're often unprepared for when they come our way. Once you reap the rewards of success, it starts to feel very good. Unfortunately, that feeling can build on itself in a very negative way. At some point, if you're successful for long enough (or got it through no efforts of your own), you forget what caused everyone to applaud you in the first place and start thinking that you are being praised simply because you're you.

The Doctrine of Family III

39: The Peanut Gallery Rule

Every once in a while you should ask yourself the following: Would you still be doing what you're doing if other folks could see? Would you feel comfortable divulging the evening's activities to a judge? If the answer to either of these question is "no," then you must ask yourself why. Is it merely a matter or privacy, or is something ridiculous going on?

40: Watch for the Nickel-and-Dime Effect

Nickel-and-diming ignores the cumulative effect of enjoyable wrongs that pave the way to an addiction. In order to keep this kind of small-step logic at bay, you have to make conscious decisions about the things you will not do. This list should include small destructive habits that are of specific concern to you. You have to know what kind of people you need not be around, the kind who pull you off track and make you forget what it is you've got to do. It also helps if you have a few cheats to signal an emerging nickel-and-dime concern. For instance, watch for key nickel-and-dime expressions like, "Just this once," or more dangerous yet, "One more time won't matter."

The Rules of Reconciliation

41: Show Some Passion for the Proper Things

There are a whole lot of different ways you can live any particular moment. Each one, in and of itself, is both an option and opportunity. You can fill it with worries, despair, or regret. You can spend it nursing old hurts and anger. Or you can put it to work for you. You can be productive in it—take a swing in some fight you *need* to fight, and see how far you get. You can fill it with calm or an act of love or with a simple pleasant memory. Libraries, community, worship, and conversation are all free. The context and meaning of your life is established from moment to moment. So never forget to feed your soul even when feeding the body is a difficult thing to do.

42: The Kathy Code: Wrap Your Arms Around It All

It took me 30 years to figure out what my sister *always* knew. Kathy was always enjoying herself because she was able to wrap her arms around the depth and breadth of the variety in this world. She looked for what she could find entertaining when she met up with new and different. My sister purposely courted joy, and she always understood its intrinsic value. There is something to relish in almost everything, if you take the time to find it. The problem is, we often see this kind of pleasure-searching as flighty and unnecessary, something that does not serve a real purpose in a rational world. But since our moods and feelings unwittingly dictate so much of what do, wouldn't it behoove us to cultivate the most positive attitude we can?

43: The Dumb-Luck Rule

Sometimes things do not make sense, and no matter how hard you try, all the dots will not connect. In life, there is no final scene where everyone's true motives and allegiances are divulged. There will be no point (while we're still breathing, at least) at which everything that seems random will all start making sense. This rule says that you can't get all caught up in that if you want to stay productive. Coincidences happen, dumb luck is real, and both can explain a whole lot of what goes on. Get comfortable with that and you'll feel a lot better no matter what goes wrong.

About the Author

Lynn Toler, a veteran municipal court judge, is the star of the syndicated television show *Divorce Court*. She lives in Arizona with her husband and sons. She is also the author of *Making Marriage Work: New Rules for an Old Institution*, published by Agate Bolden in 2012.